WHAT VARIETAL IS THAT?

A Beginners' Guide to the Most Important Wine Grape Varieties

DARBY HIGGS

Published 2019

Copyright 2019 by Darby Higgs.

All rights reserved. Other than brief extracts for the purpose of review no part of this publication may be reproduced without the written consent of the copyright owner.

TABLE OF CONTENTS

1. What is a Wine Variety?..5
2. Why Grape Varieties Matter................................10
3. Wine Varieties and Styles....................................13
4. White Wine Varieties...17
5. Red Wine Varieties..59
6. Appendix: Varieties by Country and Region 113
7. References..123
8. Further Information..125
9. About the Author..127

What is a Wine Variety?

We all have an instinctive idea of what a wine grape variety is, but it is worth exploring the concept more fully. As you learn more about wine, you will also come across discussions about varieites and clones. Just what are clones, and how are they related to varieties?

Firstly, let's deal with the question of language. Are we talking about varieties or varietals? Those who take a conservative approach to language argue that the word 'varietal' is an adjective, and it is incorrect to use it as a noun. However, in common usage, people very often use it as a noun when they discuss wines. I take the approach that language is fluid rather than fixed. So I tend to use the words 'variety' or 'varieties', but I don't get too hung up on the terminology.

The basic definition of a variety is that all of the individual vines in that variety are derived directly or indirectly from a single seedling. The new plants are propagated asexually from cuttings or grafts from that original mother plant, or from other vines which derive from it. Therefore, individual vines of a particular

WHAT IS A WINE VARIETY?

variety are all virtually genetically identical to each other.

Grape seeds, like the seeds of other plants, arise from sexual reproduction. Therefore, every variety has two parents, although some seeds arise from self-pollination. In the several millennia that grapes have been cultivated, untold millions of grape seeds have become seedlings. The vast majority are not cultivated. Seedlings are extremely variable in all sorts of characteristics. Only a tiny minority of seedlings give rise to a plant which is useful and will be kept and propagated as a new variety.

The majority of varieties have arisen by natural crossings where pollen is spread from one plant to another by wind or insects. This cross-pollination was more common in the past, when vineyards often consisted of several interplanted varieties rather than the more orderly arrangement today, where vineyards consist of a single variety or several blocks containing just one variety.

Over the past couple of centuries, grape varieties have been deliberately bred. Often, the breeding intention is to combine the good characteristics of two varieties into one new variety.

For example, the variety Pinotage was deliberately bred in South Africa by crossing Pinot Noir and Cinsaut. The first parent was chosen for its ability to produce fine wines; and the second, for its ability to thrive in a harsh viticultural environment. In this case, the plan

WHAT VARIETAL IS THAT?

was successful, but many thousands of Pinot Noir X Cinsaut seedlings would have been tested and found wanting before the eventual mother Pinotage plant was identified.

There is some confusion in the minds of winegrowers, winemakers and consumers, both novices and experts, about the difference between varieties and clones.

All of the plants of a grape variety are derived directly or indirectly via asexual reproduction from a single vine. So their genomes or genetic makeups are, in fact, very similar or nearly identical, but there are very small differences. Sometimes, these differences can become very important.

To find out how these differences occur, we need to look at how a grape vine (or any other plant) grows.

A plant grows by forming new cells by cell division. The genes in each new cell are copied from the mother cell, but the copying is not quite perfect. Tiny changes called mutations occur. So all of the cells of a plant don't have exactly the same genes. Most of the mutations are not noticed by the plant, let alone by the viticulturist. But some mutations can have major effects.

For example, in a vineyard in the South Australian region of Langhorne Creek, a Cabernet Sauvignon plant started producing bunches of bronze rather than dark berries on one cane. A mutation had occurred so that all of the cells in that particular arm of the vine carried a

WHAT IS A WINE VARIETY?

different gene involved in the colouring of the grapes. When cuttings were taken from that mutant arm to propagate new vines, they all produced bronze berries; and the new clone was called Malian.

Later, a further mutation on a Malian vine produced a white clone called Shalastin. Cleggett Wines now makes and markets wines from these new clones. From the consumer's point of view, they are distinct varieties; but strictly speaking, they are clones of the same variety - Cabernet Sauvignon.

More often, the mutations causing new clones to arise are more subtle than the change of berry colour. The new clone may be more vigorous in the vineyard; it may have disease resistance; or there may be slightly different compounds in the skin, giving rise to better (or worse) aromas and flavours in the wine it produces.

Viticulturists take great pains to identify and propagate from clones with desirable characteristics.

Older varieties and those that have been grown in a wide variety of viticultural environments tend to have many more recognised clones, and the clones are more diverse in their characteristics.

Why do grape varieties matter? Careful selection of the appropriate wine grape variety is critical for successful grape-growing and winemaking. Different varieties can have vastly different characteristics in the vineyard and in the wine produced.

WHAT VARIETAL IS THAT?

Consumers need to know at least something about varieties to choose wines they like. But there is much more to it than that. The grape variety is only one factor in the production of fine wine.

WHY GRAPE VARIETIES MATTER

There are thousands of different grape varieties used to make wine. About a thousand are used commercially at least somewhere in the world, around 200 are used fairly commonly, while the top ten make up about 40% of the area planted to grapes worldwide.

Wine varieties differ from each other in a large number of characteristics, which may or may not be of interest to the grape grower, the winemaker, and finally, the consumer.

Virtually every characteristic of the grape vine and the grape itself differs between varieties. Ampelographers — people skilled at vine identification — use factors such as the shape and size of shoots, leaves, bunches, individual grapes and seeds to distinguish between varieties. These characteristics are all genetically controlled, but the genes can be expressed in different ways in different environments. Grape variety identification was always a slightly inaccurate science.

WHAT VARIETAL IS THAT?

Since the mid 1990s, however, DNA profiling has been commonly used. It provides an objective method of identification and, as a bonus, it also reveals parent-offspring or sibling relationships between varieties. Thus, quite elaborate pedigrees for grape varieties can be constructed.

The most obvious difference between varieties is the skin colour of the grape. In simple terms, varieties are either red or white (really dark purple or green). In fact, there are gradations of colour — many shades of green through to quite golden-yellow skin, various pinkish-bronze colours often called gris or grey, through to various hues in the red, purple and black spectrum.

Perhaps the next most significant trait from the grape growers' point of view is the time taken for the grapes to ripen to to maturity. Some varieties ripen much earlier than others, by up to six or more weeks in some climates. Late-maturing varieties, for example, Grenache and Mourvèdre, will not ripen at all in cold wine-growing regions. Early-maturing varieties, such as Pinot Noir and Riesling, will ripen in hot climates; but grapes that ripen early in very hot conditions usually do not make good wine.

Over the centuries, grape growers have selected and propagated varieties which give high yields in their particular region. But over the past few decades, wine quality has become more important than quantity.

Grape varieties also differ widely in their susceptibility or resistance to disease. This is especially important in

WHY GRAPE VARIETIES MATTER

areas where there is summer and autumn rain, which creates conditions suitable for the spread of fungal diseases.

Until the middle of the 20th century, wine consumers knew little about grape varieties. Wine was marketed under the name of styles, regions and producers; and often, the name of merchants.

In Australia, for example, wines were frequently labelled Moselle, Hock, White Burgundy, or Chablis for whites; and Claret, Burgundy and Hermitage for reds. The names were taken from European regions, and were supposed to indicate the style of wine. The similarities were approximate at best.

Now, the name of variety is now prominently displayed on the label, and consumers are much more aware of grape varieties.

There are downsides to varietal labelling. Less sophisticated wine drinkers are really more interested in the style of wine than the varietal composition. Not all wines made from a particular variety taste similar.

Varietal labelling also does little to inform about whether a wine is dry, off-dry or sweet. Another problem is that varietal labelling leads many consumers to think that straight varietal wines are somehow superior to blends.

WINE VARIETIES AND STYLES

In the new world we are so accustomed to seeing wines bearing varietal names that we sometimes fall into the trap of thinking some other words commonly use on wine labels are names of grape varieties. Here are a few words that occasionally need clarification. This is especially important as international agreements are phasing out

Bordeaux and Burgundy are two regions of France, both best known for producing red wine but both regions make impressive whites as well.

Red Burgundy is almost invariably Pinot Noir. The term Burgundy was also used to describe a style of red wine supposedly softer than Claret. Australian sparkling red was was previously labelled "Sparkling Burgundy" even though it most commonly made from Shiraz.

White Burgundy is made in the eponymous region from Chardonnay grapes, but the term was applied to medium bodied white wines elsewhere, for example in

WINE VARIETIES AND STYLES

Western Australia where it was made from a blend of Verdelho and Chenin Blanc

Red Bordeaux is made from a half dozen or so varieties Cabernet Sauvignon, Merlot, Cabernet Franc, Petit Verdot, Malbec and Carmenere. Both varietal and blends of two or more of these varieties are made. Claret is an old term for Bordeaux red wines that was appropriated as a generic term for dry red wines

The best known white wine style made in Bordeaux is Graves, made with Muscadelle, Semillon and Sauvignon Blanc. These same three varieties are used to make the sweet luscious wines of Sauternes and Barsac.

Chablis Strictly speaking this is a white wine made from Chardonnay in a defined AOC region in the North of Burgundy. In the past the term was used in the New World to describe the style of steely dry white wine regardless of its origin or varietal composition. Modern naming rules have largely eliminated this misuse.

Hermitage is an appellation in the northern Rhone region. Red Hermitage is made from the Shiraz grape. White Hermitage is made from the Marsanne grape and sometimes Roussanne. The name Hermitage has been used in the past as a synonym for Marsanne in Switzerland, Cinsaut in South Africa, and Shiraz in Australia. The name Hermitage was formerly used to describe a style of dry red wine, rather than wine from that region. Penfold's Grange was called Grange

WHAT VARIETAL IS THAT?

Hermitage for many years. In more recent times 'Hermitage has been dropped form the name.

For many years the word 'Champagne' was used for any sparkling wine regardless of its origin. Nowadays if you find the word on a label it probably means that the wine comes from the Champagne region, but the transition to accuracy is not quite complete. Sparkling wines from other areas of the world shouldn't be called Champagne. In France such wines are called Cremant, in Spain Cava, in Italy Spumante. You will often see the word Brut on sparkling wine. It means something like crude or raw, brutish even. It indicates the wine is not sweetened or it has very low residual sugars. Another term commonly found on sparkling wine labels is Cuvee. It means different things in different contexts. It might mean just batch or it might mean special selected batch. It is perhaps more of a marketing word than a word derived from wine.

A few Italian wine styles and regions can be mistaken for varietal names. Barolo and Barbaresco, are two villages in the Piedmont Region which give their names to highly regarded DOCG wines made from the Nebbiolo variety. Chianti is a region in Tuscany rather than a grape variety, Brunello di Montalcino is a region whose wine is made from a particular clone of Sangiovese. Vino Nobile de Montepulciano is wine made from Sangiovese and named after the town of Montepulciano, not the grape variety Montepulciano.

WINE VARIETIES AND STYLES

Chianti is a wine region in central Tuscany. Chianti Classico is defined region in the centre of Chaianti. The red wines from here are made predominately from Sangiovese, some have small amounts of the varieties Mammolo and Canaiolo blended in.

Soave is the name of a region Veneto, northern Italy. It gives its name to the dry white wines made from Garganega, Pinot Blanc, Chardonnay and Trebbiano.

Rioja is a wine region in North Central Spain, most notable for its red wines, based on Tempranillo and/or Grenache sometimes blended with Graciano. Four levels of Rioja are made - Joven, designed to be consumed young, Crianza aged for a year in oak and two in bottle, Reserva aged for a year in Oak and two in the bottle and Gran Reserva released after two years in oak and three in bottle. Reserva and Gran Reserva are only made in good vintage years.

Port was once used widely as a generic term for sweet fortified red wines similar to those made in Porto, Portugal. In Portugal these fortified wines are made from a mixture of quite a few red wine varieties.

WHITE WINE VARIETIES

Here are some wine grape varieties that you should know about. Some of them will be unfamiliar, but just about everyone will be able to find a bottle or two with a little searching.

They have been selected mainly off the basis of their popularity, but I have used some professional judgment (read: personal bias) in selecting what was in and what was out.

I have also used my personal preferences as to the naming of the varieties. Mostly, I have used the official or prime name, but this is sometimes a matter of opinion and and depends on where in the world you are located. I don't think many Argentinians use the prime name Cot, but that is arguably the correct name for Malbec.

The information on the origin of each of the varieties is based mainly on Wine Grapes by Jancis Robinson, Julia Harding and Jose Vouillamoz. The naming of grape varieties is often an area of contention, but modern research and DNA analysis is disentangling the mismatch between the facts and the myths about old varieties.

WHITE WINE VARIETIES

The rank of each variety is derived from Which Winegrape Varieties are Grown Where? by Kym Anderson of the University of Adelaide. This ranking reflects the relative importance of the variety according to the area planted globally.

I have included some elementary food suggestions for each wine. These are by no means prescriptive or exhaustive; rather, they are intended to suggest the style of wine commonly made from the variety.

Albarino
al-bah-REEN-yoh
(Origin: Portugal, Rank: 103, Prime name: Alvarinho)
Aromas and flavours: Peaches, apricots, apples, lemon, grapefruit.
Similar varieties: Pinot Blanc, Riesling, Pinot Grigio, Godello.

Albarino makes fresh crisp whites in Northern Portugal and the adjacent Spanish region of Galicia, especially in the Rias Baixas DO. In Portugal, it is called Alvarinho. In both places, it is used to make varietal wines; but in Portugal, it is also commonly blended with other varieties, most notably Loureiro, to make Vinho Verde.

From the turn of the 21st century, Albarino has become fashionable in other wine regions, for example, in California, Oregon and Washington State; and in New Zealand.

WHAT VARIETAL IS THAT?

In the early noughties, an attempt was made to introduce Albarino into Australia. A significant number of wineries planted vines from a supposedly reputable source in the belief they were Albarino. However, in 2009, doubts about the true identity of these vines were confirmed — the variety was actually Savagnin. Some growers persisted with Savagnin as they had already proved it makes excellent wine. More recently, 'true' Albarino has been produced by several Australian wineries.

Albarino wines are delicately flavoured. They are probably best made without oak, and consumed while young.

Food choices: The crispness of these wines goes well with seafood-based tapas, grilled sardines, or gazpacho. You can also try Albarino with Japanese food such as tempura.

Assyrtiko
ah-SEER-tee-koh
(Origin: Greece, Rank: 282)
Aromas and flavours: Minerals, lemon, lime, apples.
Similar varieties: Riesling, Torrontés, Gewürztraminer (without the floral aromas).

This variety is native to the Greek island of Santorini, where the terroir is extreme. There is no soil as such on the island. It is covered with a loose mixture of pumice pebbles, sand, volcanic ash, and rocks from solidified lava. There is no clay to bind this together. The rainfall

WHITE WINE VARIETIES

of 400mm is inadequate for vines to grow unassisted, and there are no water resources on the island for irrigation. The saviour is the sea mist, which is soaked up by the hygroscopic 'soil'. Just to make traditional viticulture more difficult, there are no native trees on the island for trellising posts. Rather, the vines are trained into baskets on the ground.

In these circumstances, a tough variety is needed; and Assyrtiko fits the bill nicely. The wines are usually crisp and austere with a strong structure and subtle aromatics.

In recent years, Jim Barry Wines in the Clare Valley of South Australia has pioneered the variety. Their 2017 Assyrtiko was awarded a Gold Medal at the Australian Alternative Varieties Wine Show.

Food choices: Start with a Greek salad. Assyrtiko is robust enough to complement the creamy sharpness of feta cheese. In fact, the steely structure of Assyrtiko wines won't be overwhelmed by any tart foods such as olives, yogurt, or citrus-flavoured dishes. It is also one of a few varieties which pair well with mildly spiced Indian food.

Arneis
ahr-NAYSS
(Origin: Italy, Rank: 252)
Aromas and flavours: Honey, herbs, apples, pears, citrus, honeysuckle.
Similar varieties: Pinot Blanc, Cortese.

Arneis is native to the Piedmont region of Northwest Italy, and little is found outside that region apart from small amounts in Liguria and Sardinia.

The history of this variety follows a similar trajectory to that of Viognier. It was an obscure variety in just a few Piedmontese vineyards; and was often just blended in with Nebbiolo, just like Viognier is co-fermented with Shiraz. One theory about its survival is that winegrowers left a few Arneis vines in their vineyards as they were sweeter and attracted birds away from the more valuable Nebbiolo.

In the early 1980s, the fortunes of this variety were revived in Piedmont; and more winemakers started to make white wines with Arneis rather than using it to soften Nebbiolo.

Outside of Italy, Australia is the only country where Arneis has taken off. It is used successfully in many cooler Australian regions. There are small amounts in California and Oregon.

Arneis wines tend to have subtle honey and white-fruit aromas and flavours. They are low in acid, and hence, best enjoyed young.

Food choices: Pair these wines with Italian antipasto, or pasta with less assertive sauces. The subtle flavours of Arneis go well with delicate dishes such as tempura and fried zucchini flowers. Their low acidity also makes them suitable for serving as an aperitif.

Chardonnay
shar-duh-NAY
(Origin: France, Rank: 5)
Aromas and flavours: Apples, butterscotch, citrus, tropical fruits, vanilla.
Similar varieties: Semillon, Pinot Blanc, Aligote.

This is the world's most widely planted white wine variety if we discount Airén, the Spanish variety which is mostly used for distillation into brandy. Virtually every wine-producing country has some Chardonnay; hence, it is often referred to as an international variety, even though its origin is almost certainly in Burgundy.

DNA analysis indicated that it arose from a crossing of Pinot with the now-rare variety Gouais Blanc. In turn, Chardonnay is a parent of several other varieties.

Chardonnay is a controversial variety in that it makes some of the best as well as some of the worst wines. In some ways, it is a victim of its own versatility. In hot regions, Chardonnay yields very highly under irrigation.

WHAT VARIETAL IS THAT?

This leads to industrial-scale production. The problem is that wines made under these conditions are seldom much good, and they are frequently further degraded by the overuse of wood.

In cooler areas, such as Burgundy and Chablis, Chardonnay makes extremely attractive wines. Some of them, like the famed white Burgundies, are also very expensive. These wines tend to have good body with a buttery texture, but without the extremes of high levels of phenolics found elsewhere.

Chardonnay's other starring role is in Champagne, where it is used to make the eponymous sparkling wine. Sometimes, it is used alone to make Blanc de Blanc, but more often it is blended with Pinot Noir or Pinot Meunier to make Champagne. Many other wine regions around the world use a similar varietal mix to make sparkling wines, but of course they can't call these wines Champagne nowadays.

Food choices: Chardonnay wines tend to be medium- to full-bodied, so they are well suited to roast chicken, white meats with cream-based sauces, and rich seafood dishes such as crayfish or smoked fish.

Chenin Blanc

Shen-inn BLAHN
(Origin: France, Rank: 26)
Aromas and flavours: Honey, apples pears, flowers, citrus, chamomile, peaches, quinces.
Similar varieties: Verdelho.

This is a versatile variety hailing from the middle reaches of France's Loire Valley, where it makes a range of different white wine styles. The most famous manifestation is in the wines of the Vouvray AOC, which can be sparkling or still, dry, off-dry, moelleux (semi-sweet), or sweet. Some of the richer Chenin Blanc wines from the Loire are extremely suitable for ageing. This is one of a few white wine varieties which is capable of producing wines that will last several decades.

Chenin Blanc is grown in several areas in France outside the Loire Valley, but the largest plantings are in South Africa. In the hot areas of this country, Chenin Blanc was able to thrive and produce huge yields of neutral-tasting wine. Some of it was distilled for spirits, much of it was blended with other white wine varieties, and a large amount was used for cheap plonk. Nowadays, quite a few South African winemakers are taking the variety seriously and making quality wine, but the reputation of the variety is still very low.

In Australia, a similar story played out. Chenin Blanc was grown in warm to hot areas, especially in Western Australia, and often used for blending. For example, it used to comprise a major part of the famous Houghton's

"White Burgundy". Much less is grown now, but a few enthusiastic growers and winemakers realise the value of this superb variety.

Food choices: Sparkling Chenin can be used for any occasion where you could imagine serving Champagne. Dry Chenin is great with dishes such as roast pork with apple sauce, poultry and smoked trout. Sweeter Chenin wines can be paired with fruit-based desserts, say, tarte Tatin.

Colombard

co-lum-BAHRD
(Origin: France, Rank: 32)
Aromas and flavours: Flowers, lemons, nectarines, often quite neutral flavours.
Similar varieties: Albarino, Trebbiano, Semillon.

In France, Colombard is grown mainly in the southwest. It is also grown in California and other American states, as well as in South Africa and Australia. Plantings are declining rapidly in all of these places.

This variety is most commonly grown for distillation into Armagnac, Brandy and Cognac. It tends to yield well, but the wines are often low in acidity but high in alcohol. The former trait makes the variety suitable for low-quality wines; the latter is desirable for distilling purposes.

The wines that are not distilled are often quite bland. Hence, they are commonly blended with other white varieties to make bulk wines. However, there are a few examples where enthusiastic winemakers are able to conjure some very attractive and flavourful wines from Colombard.

Food choices: The everyday drinking wines made from Colombard can be enjoyed with sweet and sour Chinese dishes, or milder Thai cuisine.

Cortese
kor-TAY-zee
(Origin: Italy, Rank: 148)
Aromas and flavours: Aromatic citrus, citrus flowers, melons, greengage plums, herbs.
Similar varieties: Arneis, Savagnin.

This variety is from the Piedmont region of Northern Italy. Cortese is a controversial variety with passionate admirers and critics. At best, it makes mildly aromatic wines in the Gavi DOCG with rich flavours, but there are many lesser wines also made.

There are just a couple of producers of this wine in Australia. Hidden Valley in the Upper Goulburn Region of Central Victoria pioneered the variety, with quite some success.

Food choices: The crisp wines made from this variety can be paired with grilled seafood. More opulent Cortese wines such as Gavi are suitable for more elaborate seafood dishes.

Fiano
Fee-AH-noh
(Origin: Italy, Rank: 222)
Aromas and flavours: Honey, apples, flowers, hazelnuts, herbs.
Similar varieties: Greco.

This variety is grown in the Campania Region and, to lesser extent, in other Central and Southern Italian regions, including Sicily. Its most famous expression is the Fiano di Avellino DOCG from the region near Naples.

Fiano was introduced into Australia just a decade or so ago; and is now producing some stunning wines, especially in South Australia. It is clearly the most outstanding success of the recent trend in Australia of importing varieties from the warmer southern half of Italy.

Fiano wines are rich, fragrant and medium-bodied, sometimes with a waxy texture. The weight of these wines are somewhat lighter than Viognier or Chardonnay, but generally much heavier than Sauvignon Blanc or Vermentino. The variety also has the ability to retain its acidity in warm climates. This, combined with the rich flavours, means that the wines have ageing potential, if you can be patient.

Food choices: The fuller-bodied wines made from Fiano are very suitable for pairing with richer seafood dishes or with roast chicken. Try it with tiella — Puglian-style mussel and potato casserole.

Friulano
free-oo-LAH-noh
(Origin: France, Rank: 117, Prime name: Sauvigonasse)
Aromas and flavours: Peaches, pears, green apples, almonds.
Similar varieties: Muscadelle, Riesling, Sauvignon Blanc.

This variety is a naming pedant's nightmare. It originated in France's Gironde region, where it is called Sauvigonasse even though it is not related to Sauvignon Blanc. In the 2012 book Wine Grapes, the rule is that the prime name of variety is that given in the area where the grape originated. The rule in this case is not very apt as the variety is hardly present in France. In Northern Italy, it was formerly grown under the name of Tocai Friuliano or variations of it. Of course, this upset the Hungarians, so the Tocai part of the name has been dropped with varying degrees of reluctance.

But behind this mess of naming, Friulano is a very good variety. It is grown in Northern Italy, especially in the Friuli region, and in neighbouring areas of Central and Eastern Europe. There are considerable areas in Chile where it is often interplanted with and confused with Sauvignon Blanc. It is also grown in Argentina and, to a lesser extent, in Australia.

The wines made from this variety are light-bodied and mildly aromatic. They often are low in acid, and are not well suited to ageing.

Food choices: Friuli is home to some of the best prosciutto, and a plate of it is a good accompaniment to wines from this variety. The low-acid, mildly aromatic style of wines made from this variety are also quite enjoyable without food.

Garganega
Gar-GAH-neh-gah
(Origin: Italy, Rank: 50)
Aromas and flavours: Lemon, ginger, almonds, pears.
Similar varieties: Pinot Grigio, Pinot Blanc.

Under its name of Garganega, this variety thrives in several regions of Northern Italy. It's best-known manifestation is as the major component of Soave, but it is also present in many blended white wines in surrounding regions.

Soave is a dry white Italian wine from the Veneto region in Northeast Italy, principally around the city of Verona. It is based on Garganega, but may it include some Trebbiano or Chardonnay.

Gargenega is also grown extensively in Sicily under the name Grecanico Dorato, or just Grecanico. Garganega is not grown much outside Italy, but there are now a few vineyards with it in Australia.

WHITE WINE VARIETIES

The vine is very vigorous and productive; and in the past, its popularity rested on its high yields rather than the quality of the wine. In more recent years, growers and winemakers have restricted the yields and make some more serious wines with Garganega, but it may take time for the reputation of the variety to outgrow its reputation for making dull and thin wines.

Food choices: Light and crisp wines go well with seafood antipasto. Better examples of Garganega wines might be good with Spaghetti Vongole (spaghetti with clams).

Gewürztraminer
Guh-VERTZ-trah-mee-ner
(Origin: Germany, Rank: 53)
Similar varieties: Riesling, Pinot Gris (but it is far more aromatic than these), Savagnin, Torrontés.
Aromas and flavours: Highly aromatic, roses, lychees, spices, herbs, ginger.

This variety is in fact a mutation of Savagnin, but it is sufficiently different for it to be regarded as a separate variety. It first appeared in the early 19th century. The 'gewürz' part of the name derives from the German word for spice, and refers to the spicy aroma of the wines.

It is widely grown throughout Europe, North and South America, and Australasia.

Gewürztraminer is a much misunderstood variety. Too many wine drinkers equate "sweet" with inferior. Hence, they routinely eschew wine like rosé and Riesling, assuming the wine is sweet just by looking at the colour or the varietal name on the label. In the case of Gewürztraminer, it is the aroma that convinces them that the wine is sweet, and therefore not worth tasting.

In fact, Gewürztraminer is often dry, or at least off-dry. It is commonly made as a varietal wine; however, it is also used in blends where a small proportion of this variety can add a lift to otherwise neutral wines. In Alsace, it is blended with Riesling and Pinot Gris to make the excellent Gentil-style dry white.

Food choices: The richness and backbone of this wine stands up to the robust flavours in soft aromatic cheese, foie gras, and Asian (especially Thai) dishes. Or try it with fruit-based desserts.

Godello
goh-DAY-oh
(Origin: Spain, Rank: 225)
Aromas and flavours: Apples, quinces, flowers, citrus, grassy.
Similar varieties: Albarino, Fiano, Verdejo.

Godello is yet another grape variety that has been rescued from obscurity and possible extinction by a group of enthusiasts in its native region of Galicia, Northwest Spain.

Its provenance overlaps that of the red wine variety Mencia. The enthusiasts of these two varieties say that wines from this region are made by God(ello) and Men(cia).

In terms of area planted, Godello is not a major variety. It makes that up in quality, but some recent experience is that it has suffered from its popularity, outstripping the value of the wine produced. At best, Godello wines are richly flavoured and well-structured, suitable for barrel and bottle ageing.

Food choices: Octopus is a Galician specialty, and a well-structured Godello might be what you need to match the flavours of grilled octopus.

Greco
GREH-koh
(Origin: Italy, Rank: 546)
Aromas and flavours: Minerals, herbs, apricots, peaches.
Similar varieties: Savagnin, Cortese.

This is another of those Southern Italian varieties that some people imagine have a Greek origin, which is quite understandable in this case. There are in fact a couple of separate varieties with this name. The variety is also called Greco di Tufo, but this is a little confusing as there is a DOCG region with that name. Greco Bianco is a distinct variety, and there are several varieties called Greco Nera.

Greco is native to the Italian region of Campania. It has recently been discovered that it is genetically identical to Asprinio from the same region, but previously thought to be a different variety.

Little of this variety is grown outside of Southern Italy, but several wineries in Australia are now making Greco wines.

Wines made from Greco can be full-bodied and aromatic. It is used for varietal wines, and also in blends with other Southern Italian varieties.

Food choices: Try this wine with Pizza Margherita. The aroma of the wine will combine with the flavours of the tomatoes, basil and mozzarella for an authentic Neapolitan meal.

Grillo
GREEL-oh
(Origin: Sicily, Rank: 103)
Aromas and flavours: Aromatic, almonds, lemon, floral.
Similar varieties: Insolia, Slankamenka.

Grillo is the variety of choice for making high-alcohol wines to make Sicily's famed fortified wine Marsala.

Like other fortified wines, Marsala has suffered a decades-long decline in popularity. Therefore, Grillo is now used more often to produce moderately aromatic, crisp, dry white wines with good structure. Plantings of this variety in Sicily are increasing rapidly as a result of its vigour in the vineyard and its ability to produce fashionable crisp dry whites.

There are no significant areas of this variety outside Italy. Attempts to introduce this variety in Australia hit a snag when it was found that most of the vines planted were in fact an obscure Balkan variety Slankamenka, in circumstances similar to the early attempts to introduce Albarino.

Grillo wines are full-bodied and slightly aromatic.

Food choices: The crisp acidity of these wines can be paired with fried seafood dishes, or perhaps with Sicilian favourite Pasta alla Norma (a rich eggplant-based sauce).

Grüner Veltliner
GROO-ner FELT-lee-ner
(Origin: Austria, Rank: 41)
Aromas and flavours: White pepper, peaches, pears, celery, melon.
Similar varieties: Riesling.

This high-quality white wine variety makes up over a third of the vineyard area in Austria. It is also grown extensively in nearby countries of Central Europe.

Grüner Veltliner has rapidly gained popularity in South Australia's Adelaide Hills Region, thanks to the pioneering work of the Hahndorf Hill Winery that has persuaded and cajoled dozens of their neighbours to grow and vinify the variety.

A versatile variety, Grüner Veltliner can make crisp dry whites for early consumption or, if picked a little later, it makes richer dry white styles with potential for ageing. Off-dry and medium-bodied wines are also made. It is most commonly used as a straight varietal.

Food choices: Its Austrian homeland suggests Wiener schnitzel, but the firm acidity copes well with mildly spiced Asian foods. Not many wines marry well with asparagus or artichokes: Grüner Veltliner is one exception.

Inzolia

inn-SOHL-yah
(Origin: Sicily, Rank: 98)
Aromas and flavours: Aromatic, almonds, flowers, peaches, citrus.
Similar varieties: Grillo, Greco.

This variety originated in Sicily where it is widely used, but it is also grown in Tuscany under the name of Ansonica. It is not grown to any extent outside Italy.

For many years, Inzolia's main role was making base wines for Marsala. But in more recent times, it is more commonly used as a varietal, or in blends for making crisp dry white wines.

WHITE WINE VARIETIES

Food choices: A Sicilian favourite for pairing for this variety is arancini. The firm acidity of these wines could also go with Thai fish cakes.

Malvasia
mahl-vah-ZEE-uh
(Origin: Italy, or somewhere in the Mediterranean)

No serious work about varieties can omit mention of Malvasia. The problem is what to say about it in less than 10,000 words. Firstly, it isn't a single variety, but a whole collection of varieties of various colours, most of which are not genetically or even viticulturally related. In fact, in her book Wine Grapes, Jancis Robinson lists 22 varieties with Malvasia in the prime name; and there are at least 60 other varieties known by synonyms including the word Malvasia or a near-derivative. This indicates that most of these varieties are old and have been grown in areas where viticulture has operated on a traditionally small scale.

The name is thought to derive from the Greek port Monemvasia, famous as a trading hub for wine. But genetic analysis suggests that few of the various Malvasia varieties are related to other Greek varieties, or to each other.

So what can I confidently say about Malvasia wine? It will be either white, (most commonly) pink or red; it may be fortified or not; it may be sweet or dry, or something in between. The wines made from these varieties are often sweet fortified styles, 'Malmsey', for example. Unfortified Malvasia wines are mostly everyday drinking styles best enjoyed in the region they are produced. However, there are a few passionate winemakers who manage to conjure up something special from one or other of the Malvasia varieties.

Food choices: Dry white wines can be enjoyed with seafood-based appetisers or with white meats, generally. The sweeter fortified wines can be enjoyed with cakes at afternoon tea time, or with cream-based desserts.

Marsanne
Mahr-SAHN
(Origin: France, Rank: 194)
Aromas and flavours: Baked apples, almonds, flowers, apricots, peaches, honey, melon.
Similar varieties: Roussanne.

This is a versatile and high-quality white wine variety from the Rhone region. It is also grown in other regions in the south of France.

The Tahbilk winery in Central Victoria, Australia, had the largest plantings of this variety for many years in the middle of the 20th century, but it is now much more widely grown throughout Australia. Marsanne is also grown in California, Italy and Switzerland, where it is prized as a sweet wine.

Generally, Marsanne wines tend to be medium-bodied. They are generally not given oak treatment. This variety is also used occasionally for sparkling wine.

WHITE WINE VARIETIES

Marsanne and Roussanne are often compared. They are closely related and frequently blended, with or without a contribution of Viognier, another Rhone white.

Most white wines are best consumed young, but this is not necessarily true of Marsanne. Young wines from this variety often have a refreshing crispness, but with some bottle age, say five to eight years, the wines become much more complex, developing baked-apple or nutty flavours.

Food choices: Younger wines are typically crisp and light, and pair well with seafood antipasto such as fried whitebait. Older Marsanne wines are better with richer foods, chicken liver pate, roast veal or mature cheese.

Müller-Thurgau
MYEW-ler TOOR-goh
(Origin: Germany, Rank: 37)
Aromas and flavours: Peaches, apples, flowers.
Similar varieties: Riesling, Silvaner.

This is a deliberately bred German variety from the 19th century. Recent DNA research has shown it is a not a cross of Riesling and Silvaner, as originally thought, but a cross of Riesling and a now-extinct variety called Madeleine Royale.

Müller-Thurgau yields very well, especially in cool climates, hence its popularity. The downside is that it often produces poor-quality wines, in particular, the bland sweet wines exported en masse from Germany in the 1970s and 1980s.

This variety is widely distributed in the cooler wine regions of the world, notably New Zealand. Perhaps the most successful wines are not from its German homeland, but from the Alto Adige region in Northern Italy.

Food choices: These wines are typically rather neutral in flavour. You could serve them with poached trout. or perhaps with a cheesecake.

Muscadelle
(Origin: France, Rank: 199)
Aromas and flavours: Rich and sweet like Muscat, but with a subtle difference.
Similar varieties: While there is some similarity in name and flavour, it is not related to the various Muscat varieties.

This variety is grown in Bordeaux and in neighbouring areas of Southwest France. It is used there for blending to make sweet and dry wines, especially Sauternes and Barsac. Near Bergerac on the Dordogne River, it is used for the highly regarded Monbazillac off-dry white wine. In California, there is a small amount grown under the name of Sauvignon Vert.

In Australia, the variety was known for over a century as Tokay, under the mistaken belief it was from Hungary. It is the variety used to make what we used to call

Liqueur Tokay. Trade agreements now mean that we can't call it that. Now, it is sold under the clumsy and opaque name of Topaque. Maybe we should just call it Liqueur Muscadelle, which is what it is.

Muscadelle is also used to make dry white wines.

Food choices: The sweeter styles are suitable partners for dark chocolate, ice cream, and Christmas pudding.

Palomino
pal-uh-MEE-noh
(Origin: Spain, Rank: 38, Prime name: Palomino Fino)
Aromas and flavours: Often quite bland, but with aromas of apples and almonds.
Similar varieties: Semillon.

This is the variety most famously used to make Sherry in Andalusia, and Sherry lookalikes in many other warm to hot wine regions around the world. In some areas, it was used to make wine for distillation into brandy, but this has become less common in recent years. On the Canary Islands, it is known under the name Listan Blanco and used to make white wines.

Palomino's ability to produce high yields in hot irrigation districts prompted its use to make bulk wine used in blends with more aromatic and flavourful varieties. Some producers make sweet botrytised wines.

As noted, this variety's main role is to to make Sherry or Sherry-style wines. Fino Sherry is the driest and palest of these types. Amontillado is also very dry, but is allowed to oxidise a little and develops a light brown colour and nutty aromas. Olorosso is also dry and has a darker colour. Sometimes, it is blended with sweet sherry to make medium or cream sherry. Sweet sherries are most often made with Pedro Ximénez grapes.

Food choices: Mussels steamed in sherry, smoked almonds as an appetiser, tapas such as chorizo or seafood and mayonnaise.

Pedro Ximénez

PEHD-roh hee-MEH-nehth
(Origin: Spain, Rank: 76)
Aromas and flavours: Figs, nuts, oranges, treacle.
Similar varieties: There is an Argentine variety called Pedro Giménez, which is unrelated despite the similar name. It is used to make undistinguished white wines.

This Pedro Ximénez makes distinctive, very dark, very sweet fortified wines.

Some producers use Pedro Ximénez to make unfortified sweet botrytised wines. It is also used to add sweetness to other fortified and unfortified wines.

Food choices: This is a variety for those with a sweet tooth. Try some with grilled figs drizzled with honey. To pay homage to its Spanish origin, you could try some with Churros dipped in chocolate.

WHITE WINE VARIETIES

Petit Manseng
(Origin: France, Rank: 228)
Aromas and flavours: Apples, pears, peaches, honey
Similar varieties: Pinot Gris.

This variety is noted for its role in Southwest France, where it produces the dry or sweet and opulent wines of Jurancon and Pacherenc du Vic-Bilh. There is a related variety called Gros Manseng with bigger berries and higher yields, but the wines are not as highly regarded.

Petit Manseng is also grown to a limited extent in the Basque region of Spain, where it is sometimes a component of the local crisp dry white Chacolí.

Food choices: The wines from this variety are not shy. You can try them with steamed asparagus or Vietnamese-style stir-fried prawns.

Pinot Blanc
PEE-noh BLAHN
(Origin: France, Rank: 52)
Aromas and flavours: Pears, peaches, honey, flowers, citrus.
Similar varieties: Pinot Grigio, Chardonnay.

Pinot Blanc is closely associated with Alsace, where it is commonly blended with other white varieties. It is also an important variety in Northeastern Italy under the name Pinot Bianco. There are also significant amounts grown in Eastern Europe, the West Coast of the US and Canada. Small amounts are grown in Australia.

WHAT VARIETAL IS THAT?

This is the poor relation of the various Pinots. That is not to say there are not any very good Pinot Blanc wines around; it is just that no cult following has developed for this variety in contrast to what has happened to its near-relative relative Pinot Gris.

Pinot Blanc wines are often well-structured and lightly aromatic. Sparkling whites are also made with this variety, for example, Crémant d'Alsace.

Food choices: these wines can be successfully paired with dishes such as quiche Lorraine or rabbit in white wine sauce.

Pinot Gris/Grigio
PEE-noh GREE, PEE-noh GREE-jyoh
(Origin: France, Rank: 19, a.k.a. Pinot Grigio)
Aromas and flavours: Gris styles are aromatic with peaches, honey, pears and apricots. Grigio styles are more acidic, with citrus and mineral flavours at the fore. Similar varieties: Pinot Blanc.

This is an increasingly popular variety with two names and two identities. It is, in fact, not a variety but a mutation of Pinot Noir. The two names Gris and Grigio are from the French and Italian words for grey. This refers to the colour of the grapes: neither red nor green, but really a bronze colour. Gris and Grigio also refer, approximately at least, to the two styles of wine: the first luscious and peachy, the latter crisp and fresh. There is a spectrum of variation between the two styles.

WHITE WINE VARIETIES

In recent decades, there has been an explosion of interest in this variety, especially from those from Italy. Many other wine countries are jumping on the bandwagon as consumers can't seem to get enough of the easy-drinking, light-bodied dry whites.

Pinot Gris is most commonly used as a straight varietal; but in Alsace, it is often blended with Riesling and Gewürztraminer. It is sometimes used to make sparkling wine.

Food choices: The richer Alsatian-style Pinot Gris can be enjoyed with Kugelhopf, the local raisin and almond cake. For the crisper Italian styles, you might consider a seafood risotto.

Prosecco (a.k.a. Glera)
proh-SEHK-koh
(Origin: Italy, Rank: 42)
Aromas and flavours: Peaches.
Similar varieties: Pinot Grigio, Müller-Thurgau.

The naming of this variety is controversial. Prosecco can mean the style or the grape variety; or in fact three genetically distinct grape varieties, depending on your commercial interests and legal advice. 'Glera' is the term for the variety some Italian producers and marketers are using to try to protect the name 'Prosecco'.

This variety is grown extensively in the Veneto region in Northeast Italy. It is most commonly used to make sparkling or lightly sparkling frizzante-style wines.

WHAT VARIETAL IS THAT?

These wines have become increasingly popular as an alternative to Champagne. In recent years, many Australian winemakers have started making the variety.

Prosecco is in fact quite a versatile variety. It can be used alone or in blends to make still white wines or sweet passito styles.

Food choices: Prosecco wines are typically low in alcohol, so they are great to drink just as an aperitif. You can make the famous Bellini cocktail by adding peach puree or nectar to Prosecco. This is one wine that doesn't always need food, but you can try it with appetisers, or perhaps with a Pavlova dessert.

Riesling
REE-sling
(Origin: Germany, Rank: 18)
Aromas and flavours: Citrus (especially lime), peaches, apples, minerals.
Similar varieties: Albarino.

This variety originated in Germany, and that country still has the most vineyard areas devoted to it. It is also important in the French region of Alsace, but there is little elsewhere in France. Riesling is popular in the other wine countries of Central and Eastern Europe.

The reputation of Riesling suffered greatly in the 1960s, '70s and '80s because of the huge quantities of cheap sweet wines marketed under that name.

WHITE WINE VARIETIES

Food choices: This is a versatile wine, with the backbone to match it with grilled seafood, coq au Riesling, and lemon meringue pie.

Rkatsiteli
ar-kat-sit-TELL-ee
(Origin: Georgia, Rank: 16)
Aromas and flavours: Citrus, apples, apricots.

Rkatsiteli is regarded as one of the oldest varieties in the former Soviet republic of Georgia, which claims to have the world's oldest wine industry. It is the most widely planted variety there; and is an important player in Russia, the Ukraine, Moldova, Romania and Bulgaria. There is a small amount grown in New York State.

This is a winter-hardy variety that is popular due to its ability to retain acidity while achieving high sugar levels. It is used to make sweet, dry and sparkling wines.

Food choices: Try a dry Rkatsiteli with a classic Eastern European dish: stuffed cabbage leaves.

WHAT VARIETAL IS THAT?

Roussanne
roo-SAHN
(Origin: France, Rank: 192)
Aromas and flavours: Pears, herbs, honeysuckle, spring blossoms, citrus, melon.
Similar varieties: Semillon, Marsanne.

This variety is from the Northern Rhone, where it is often grown alongside and blended with its near-relative Marsanne. It is becoming increasingly popular in other French wine regions, the US West Coast, and Canada and Australia.

In the vineyard, Roussanne has the reputation of being harder to grow than Marsanne because it is more prone to a number of pests and diseases. Roussanne wines are more aromatic and have a higher acidity than those of Marsanne.

Food choices: These moderately aromatic wines could be good with smoked chicken salad, steamed Asian dumplings.

Sauvignon Blanc
soh-vee-NYAWN Blahnk
(Origin: France, Rank: 8)
Aromas and flavours: Grassy, gooseberries, lemon, passion fruit, tropical fruits, nectarines.
Similar varieties: Savagnin Blanc, Silvaner.

This increasingly popular variety probably originated in the Loire Valley during the 18th century. It is related to

WHITE WINE VARIETIES

a number of other varieties including Savagnin Blanc, Silvaner, Petit Manseng and Verdelho. It is also a parent of Cabernet Sauvignon.

Sauvignon Blanc was formerly best known as the variety behind the Sancerre and Fume Blanc wines of the Loire Valley. But since about the turn of the 21st century, New Zealand Sauvignon Blanc has stolen the limelight. It is also grown in other regions of France; and in Chile, South Africa, Moldova, Australia and California. It is a minor variety in most other wine-producing countries.

This variety is used either as a straight varietal, and also as a blending partner for other whites. As a varietal, the wines are often very aromatic, too much so for many palates. These wines are usually light-bodied and refreshingly crisp in contrast to the heavier, wooded Chardonnay, for example.

Less well-known is Sauvignon Blanc's role in blended wines. In Bordeaux, for example, it is used to add zest and flavour to the otherwise slightly flabby Semillon. In the Dordogne Region, it plays an important role, blended with Semillon and Muscadelle to produce dry and off-dry whites such as Monbazillac.

There are two colour mutations: Sauvignon Gris and Sauvignon Rouge. Neither are widely grown.

Food choices: The strong aromatics and structure of Sauvignon Blanc won't be overwhelmed by the robust flavours of dishes such as garlic-flavoured soft cheese and artichokes baked with olive oil and anchovies.

WHAT VARIETAL IS THAT?

Savagnin Blanc
sah-vah-NYAHN Blahnk
(Origin: France, Rank: 186)
Aromas and flavours: Grapefruit, pears, lemon, honeysuckle
Similar varieties: Albarino, Grüner Veltliner, Pinot Blanc.

Some people refer to the Savagnin family of varieties, but DNA analysis shows that Savagnin is in fact a single variety with a large number of of mutations. One is the highly perfumed Gewürztraminer mentioned above. There is also a pink version, the Savagnin Rose.

In the Jura region of Eastern France, Savagnin Blanc is the variety used to make the local specialty, vin jaune or yellow wine. This wine is made in a manner similar to flor sherry, but the wine is not fortified. The variety is also used to make more conventional dry white wines. Savagnin Blanc is also grown to make dry white wines in other European regions.

Savagnin Blanc was introduced into Australia more or less by accident; see the details in the Albarino entry above. Many Australian producers persisted with the variety even after they learned that they couldn't use the more marketable name 'Albarino'. The silver lining is that there are some excellent Australian dry whites now made from it.

Food choices: With the vin jaune style you could try Arroz con mariscos - a Portuguese seafood-and-rice dish. If you have a dry white Savagnin it would go well with fried whitebait.

Semillon
SEM-ill-ohn
(Origin: France, Rank: 39)
Aromas and flavours: Apricots, quinces, honey, citrus, peaches.
Similar varieties: Chardonnay, Palomino, Trebbiano.

Semillon is the most important white wine variety in Bordeaux for sweet wines such as Sauternes and Barsac; and for dry whites, most often in 80/20 blends with Sauvignon Blanc. Other significant areas of Semillon are planted in Australia, South Africa, Chile and Argentina, with small but increasing amounts in California and Washington State.

In Australia, the variety was known as Hunter River Riesling for many years. It was made into dry white wines and marketed in a classic Riesling-style bottle. These wines, mainly from the Hunter Valley, were highly regarded as suitable for extended bottle ageing.

Varietal Semillon wines are sometimes oaked, but lighter unoaked wines are probably more popular these days. Most winemakers seem to prefer to add some Sauvignon Blanc to make a blended wine with a little more freshness.

There is a red-skinned mutation called Semillon Rose that is grown in a few scattered vineyards in South Africa and Australia.

Food choices: Brandade (a puree of salt cod, olive oil, garlic and bread) would be a good choice to accompany white styles. You could enjoy the sweeter styles with rich, creamy desserts such as crème brûlée.

Silvaner
Sill-VAH-ner
(Origin: Austria, Rank: 193)
Aromas and flavours: Pears, peaches, minerals.
Similar varieties: Riesling, Müller-Thurgau.

The name is often spelt Sylvaner outside Germany. This is one of the major varieties of Germany, and there are considerable plantings in the Alsace Region of France. Only a small amount is now grown in Austria, from where it originated. In Switzerland, it is a minor variety, but causes confusion there as it is often grown under the name Johannisburg.

The wines from this variety are usually light and rather neutral in flavour. They are best consumed young.

Food choices: You might enjoy this wine with the Alsatian dish choucroute - mixed smoked meats on a sauerkraut base.

WHITE WINE VARIETIES

Torrontés
Toe-rron-tess
(Origin: Argentina, Rank: 83)
Aromas and flavours: Very aromatic, jasmine, flowers, peaches, mango.
Similar varieties: Gewürztraminer, dry Muscat, Viognier.

There are several varieties with this name. First and foremost is Torrontés Riojano, the most important white wine variety in Argentina. There are a few others in Argentina, and another unrelated variety in Northwest Spain. This entry deals with the Torrontés Riojano, which is what most people mean when they say Torrontés.

This variety arose as a crossing of the Muscat of Alexandria with an Argentinian variety called Criolla Chica. The Muscat heritage is responsible for some of the aromatics of the wine, although Torrontés wines are nearly always dry.

Food choices: These whites have enough oomph to stand up to spicy foods, say, Thai-style chicken salad. If you want a white wine to drink with grilled beef and chimichurri sauce, Torrontés could be a good bet.

Trebbiano

Treb-BYAH-noh
(Origin: Italy, Rank: 9)
Aromas and flavours: Herbs, citrus, apples.
Similar varieties: Pinot Grigio, Garganega.

There are about half a dozen white wine varieties with the official name Trebbiano something, and quite a few with similar names as synonyms. However, when people talk about Trebbiano, they are usually talking about Trebbiano Toscano. In France, the same variety is called Ugni Blanc.

This grape variety is extremely popular worldwide because it is adaptable, vigorous and high yielding. It is really a dual-purpose grape. Large amounts are used for distilling as the base for Cognac, brandy and other spirits. It is also used to make a rather neutral dry white wine. Much of it is used, sometimes anonymously, in cheaper blends. Some winemakers treat it kindly to produce acceptable dry white wines.

Food choices: A dry white wine made from Trebbiano would be a fine choice to drink with simple fried seafood.

WHITE WINE VARIETIES

Verdejo
vehr-DAY-hoh
(Origin: Spain, Rank: 39)
Aromas and flavours: Herbs, pears, grapefruit, nutty.
Similar varieties: Sauvignon Blanc, Albillo.

Verdejo is the variety behind the well-regarded aromatic wines of the Rueda DO in Spain. It emerged from obscurity in the 1980s, and now ranks in the top 40 of grape varieties based on area grown. In Rueda, this variety is often made as a varietal, but it is occasionally blended with other Spanish white varieties and Sauvignon Blanc.

This variety is now gaining popularity in other Spanish wine regions. While there is not much grown outside Spain, there is plenty of interest in other countries, and it will become more prominent over the next few years.

Food choices: These wines are often crisp and well-structured, so they go well with herb-dominated dishes, for example, Spaghetti with pesto sauce. Perhaps you could also try Verdejo with seafood paella.

Verdelho
vehr-DEH-loh
(Origin: Portugal, Rank: 193)
Aromas and flavours: Lime, tropical fruit, nectarines.
Similar varieties: Godello, Chenin Blanc. There is an Umbrian variety called Verdello, but it is unrelated.

This variety probably originated on the Portuguese island of Madeira, where it is used to make the eponymous fortified wine. Small amounts are also grown on continental Portugal, in France and in California.

By far, the majority of the world's Verdelho is grown in Australia. Here, it is used to make dry or off-dry table wines, alone or in blends. It thrives in humid coastal areas where summer rains cause problems with other varieties. It also yields well in the hot irrigated regions of Australia's interior.

Food choices: The fortified Madeira is eminently suitable to be sipped with a rich Christmas cake, while the fruit flavours of the still wines made from Verdelho can accompany mildly spicy Chinese stir-fry dishes.

WHITE WINE VARIETIES

Vermentino
Vair-men-TEE-noh
(Origin: Italy, Rank: 78)
Aromas and flavours: Herbs, citrus, minerals, melon, almonds.
Similar varieties: Pinot Grigio, Garganega.

The habitats of this variety are the Mediterranean islands of Corsica and Sardinia, and adjacent areas of mainland France and Italy. It is frequently found under the synonyms of Pigato in Italy and Rolle in France.

Vermentino wines are generally light- to medium-bodied, and are often crisp and somewhat austere. If the grapes are allowed to ripen a little more, the wine becomes more aromatic and fruitier.

Food choices: Pissladiere — a Provençal-style onion and anchovy tart. The Sardinian connection suggests grilled sardines. This sounds a bit too neat of a coincidence, but a dish of grilled sardines is greatly enhanced by a glass of cold, crisp Vermentino.

Viognier
vee-oh-NYAY
(Origin: France, Rank: 61)
Aromas and flavours: Apricots, peaches, grapefruit, honeysuckle.
Similar varieties: Chardonnay, Torrontés.

The Viognier variety has an interesting history. Until about 50 years ago, it was on the brink of extinction. Its last enclave was in the Northern Rhone region, where just a few hectares were being used to produce Condrieu, a full-bodied but soft and perfumed white wine known only to a few cognoscenti. The secret got out, and the variety is now planted throughout the world.

It is co-fermented with Shiraz in Australia and California, and these wines became very popular in the first decade of this century. However, the best use of Viognier is when it is made into dry whites.

The style of wine made from violin varies according to the state of ripeness at vintage. Early-picked wines tend to be lighter and fresher. Later-picked wines are a darker golden colour, more aromatic and richer; and are akin to Chardonnay in weight.

Food choices: Viognier wines are typically full-bodied, and even the lighter styles demand some sort of food. The strong flavours can also hold their own with spicier foods such as chicken tagine, or mild curries.

Xarello
shah-REHL-loh
(Origin: Spain, Rank: 79)
Aromas and flavours: Citrus, pears, herbs.
Similar varieties: Chardonnay.

The name of this variety is also written as Xarel-lo. It is mostly associated with the Spanish region of Catalonia where it makes still and sparkling wines, called Cava

WHITE WINE VARIETIES

in Spain. Little is grown outside Catalonia, in Spain or elsewhere in the world.

Cava is sometimes 100% Xarello, but more often it has other Spanish varieties such as Macabeo and Parallada in the blend. Xarello is favoured because it adds structure and body to the wine.

Xarello produces powerful still dry white wines, either as a straight varietal or as a component of blends.

Food choices: As Cava, you can enjoy Xarello with a range of dishes, from appetisers to dessert. The strong structure of still white wines made with Xarello makes an ideal pairing with suquet de peix, the Catalan version of bouillabaisse.

RED WINE VARIETIES

Agiorgitiko
eye -or-YEE-tee-koh
(Origin: Greece, Rank, 149)
Aromas and flavours: Blackberries, plums, spices.
Similar varieties: Gamay, Merlot, Tempranillo.

The name means 'St George'. This is the most planted variety in Greece, where it makes a variety of red wine styles including rosé. The best known examples are from the Nemea region on the Peloponnese Peninsula. Agiorgitiko doesn't seem to generate much interest outside its homeland and the Greek diaspora.

Food choices: These wines tend to be low in acid, and are best suited to milder foods. Try them with moussaka or Greek vegetable stews.

RED WINE VARIETIES

Aglianico
ah-LYAH-nee-koh
(Origin: Italy, Rank: 69)
Aromas and flavours: Black cherries, dark chocolate, plums.
Similar varieties: Nebbiolo.

This is a deeply coloured red wine variety from the regions of Basilicata and Campania in Southern Italy. It is grown to a limed extent in Australia and California.

The name implies that it was believed to be of Greek origin (Hellenic), but recent research indicates that it originated in Italy. Aglianico Taurasi DOCG and Aglianico del Vulture DOCG are the two most highly regarded examples, the latter being grown in the volcanic slopes of Mount Vulture.

The wines from this variety are often deeply coloured and loaded with tannins, in which case they need a decade or two of bottle ageing.

Food choices: These wines are robust and age-worthy. Enjoy them with richer savoury dishes such as spicy sausages, beef or game stews. Aglianico wines are also suitable with pasta dishes with spicy meat-based sauces.

Alicante Bouschet
ah-leh-cant Boo-Shay
(Origin: France, Rank: 23, Prime name: Alicante Henri Bouschet)
Aromas and flavours: Earthy and spicy, with dark fruit aromas.
Similar varieties: Graciano.

This is an unusual red wine variety in that the pulp (flesh) of the grape is coloured. Most red wine grapes have a colourless pulp and juice, with the skin providing the colour. There are just a few exceptions for varieties such as Alicante Bouschet which have a coloured pulp and juice. These varieties are called 'Teinturier'.

Alicante Bouschet was once popular as a blending partner to add colour to cheap mass-produced wines of Spain and Southern France, but its usage for this purpose is declining rapidly. It is grown in many other wine-producing countries, but is going out of fashion in most of them.

It can be used to make varietal red wines, but only rarely are they regarded as serious wines.

In Australia, the variety is best known for its use to make a popular rosé by Rockford in the Barossa Valley.

Food choices: In view of its Spanish origins, you might pair this wine with a seafood paella, while the the rosé version would suit a platter of tapas or antipasto.

RED WINE VARIETIES

Barbera

bar-BEAR-ah
(Origin: Italy, Rank: 36)
Aromas and flavours: Blackberries, cherries, figs, herbs, plums, spicy.
Similar varieties: Sangiovese, Montepulciano.

This is a popular Northwest Italian variety that is grown in most other wine regions throughout Italy, and indeed in most other wine-producing countries. To some extent, it lives in the shadow of Nebbiolo, but Barbera is easier to grow and it makes more straightforward wines. The ability of Barbera grapes to hold their acidity in warmer climates also contributes to its popularity.

The flagship Barbera wines are from the DOCG regions of Barbera d'Alba and Barbera d'Asti, named after two towns in Piedmont.

Barbera wines are usually dark-coloured and soft. The dark colour is valued by winemakers who are looking for blending material.

There is a white wine variety called Barbera Bianca, but it is not related.

Food choices: Barbera wines are savoury and sometimes have a hint of spice; many seem to have an affinity with tomato-based sauces. So get out your Italian cookbooks for some pairing inspiration. If the ingredients of a dish include tomatoes and oregano, Barbera would be a good choice of wine.

Bastardo
— See Trousseau

Blaufränkisch
Blawh-FRANK-eessh
(Origin: Austria or Hungary, Rank: 48)
Aromas and flavours: Cherries, peppers, blackberries, spices.
Similar varieties: Pinot Noir, Zinfandel, Zweigelt, Gamay.

Blaufränkisch is grown in Austria, Hungary, and other Central and Eastern European countries. It is also found in Canada, Washington State and New York State. There are just a few plantings in Australia. Its name suggests that it is from the German region of Franconia, but this is unlikely. It is also called Limberger or Lemberger in Germany, and Kékfrankos in Hungary.

This variety can make deep rich wines if not overcropped, but it is often used to make lighter-style wines. It is treated differently in different regions so that a variety of styles are produced.

Food choices: These are often full-bodied wines with good flavours. As such, they handle strongly flavoured main-course dishes. Goulash is a favourite Middle European dish which might go well with this variety, or perhaps you could try it with roast duck and cherries.

RED WINE VARIETIES

Cabernet Franc
ka-ber-NAY FRAHNK
(Origin: Spain, Rank: 17)
Aromas and flavours: Raspberries, plums, red cherries, red currants.
Similar varieties: Gamay, Merlot, Cabernet Sauvignon, Carménère.

This variety lives in the shadow of Cabernet Sauvignon, its celebrity offspring. The other parent of Cabernet Sauvignon is Sauvignon Blanc. Although it is best known for its role in Bordeaux and the Loire, it is most likely to have originated in Spain.

Cabernet Franc is now grown in most wine regions throughout the world.

As you would expect, Cabernet Franc is quite similar to Cabernet Sauvignon, but it ripens a little earlier. Hence, it can be used in cooler regions such as the Loire Valley.

Cabernet Franc is most often used in blends with Cabernet Sauvignon and Merlot, but an increasing number of winemakers are making varietal Cabernet Franc wines. These are often light- to medium-bodied, with raspberry flavours prominent on the palate. They are well worth seeking out.

Food choices: The wines are often lighter than Cabernet Sauvignon-dominant wines. So perhaps choose veal rather than beef, or rabbit rather than wild boar. If you prefer red wine to accompany roast chicken, then Cabernet Franc might be a good choice.

Cabernet Sauvignon
ka-ber-NAY soh-vee-NYAWN
(Origin: France, Rank: 1)
Aromas and flavours: Black currants, cedar, chocolate, mint.
Similar varieties: Merlot, Tempranillo.

As the world's most popular wine grape variety, it is grown in just about every wine-producing region where the climate is warm enough to ripen it, and in a few where it is a little too cold. Huge vineyards of Cabernet Sauvignon are now being planted in China, where the variety takes up an astonishing 75% of the total vineyard area.

Cabernet Sauvignon originated in Bordeaux, the offspring of a natural cross of Cabernet Franc and Sauvignon Blanc. It is the mainstay of Bordeaux, but fine wines are being made from it around the wine world.

Cabernet Sauvignon is often used as a varietal or in blends with one or more of the other so-called Bordeaux varieties (chiefly Merlot and Cabernet Franc), but sometimes also Petit Verdot, Malbec and Carménère. Shiraz-Cabernet Sauvignon blends used to be quite common in Australia, but they are fairly rare these days. In many areas, this variety is also used as a minor component in blends, for example, with Sangiovese or with Tempranillo.

The wines tend to be deeply coloured and tannic, often quite suitable for ageing. In cold areas or in cold years, the wines tend to have unpleasant unripe capsicum flavours.

Food choices: Roasted or grilled red meats are the classic food recommendations for these wines. You can also try Cabernet Sauvignon with dark poultry such as quail, duck or squab pigeon. Old Cabernet wines can be paired with mature sharp cheeses such as pecorino.

Carignan
kar-in-YON
(Origin: Spain, Rank: 11, Prime name: Mazuelo)
Aromas and flavours: Blackberries, cherries, earthy, spices.
Similar varieties: Grenache, Mourvèdre, Bonvedro.

Despite its Spanish origin, Carignan is more commonly associated with the Languedoc region of France. It is grown in other warmer wine regions of Southern France and on the island of Sardinia, where it is called Carignano. In Spain, it is the mainstay of the wines in the Priorat DOC and other regions of Catalonia. It is grown in many other warmer vineyard areas around the world, including in Chile, where it has a reputation for serious red wines.

As a high-yielding variety, it was very popular half a century ago when quantity, rather than quality, was important. During the years of the "European wine lake", Carignan developed a reputation for producing large volumes of unattractive wine. In more recent years, the variety has developed better press, thanks in no small part to the efforts of the Carignan Renaissance movement, led by winemaker John Bojanowski, in the Minervois region of the Languedoc.

Carignan is prized as a source of acidity and tannins in blends, but it is also used to make varietal red wines and rosé.

Carignan is grown in Australia, but it is believed that some vineyards thought to be Carignan are, in fact, either Mourvèdre or Bonvedro.

There are colour mutations of this variety, giving rise to Carignan Blanc and Carignan Gris.

Food choices: This variety tends to make rustic wines with prominent acidity, so they could be paired with grilled Toulouse sausages, or Moroccan-spiced tagines.

Carménère
kar-men-AIR
(Origin: France, Rank: 62)
Aromas and flavours: Blackberries, herbs, spices, plums.
Similar varieties: Merlot, Cabernet Franc.

Originally, Carménère was (and still is) a permitted variety in Bordeaux blends. Since the Phylloxera plague in the 1870s, it has become quite rare in Bordeaux; and virtually none is grown elsewhere in France.

RED WINE VARIETIES

This variety is closely associated with Chile, where it is a major contributor. It got there via a happy accident. In the mid-19th century, many vineyards in Chile were planted to what was thought to be Merlot. It turned out that the vineyards had been planted to a mixture of Merlot and Carménère vines. Since the mid-1990s, identity has been sorted out, with many Chilean growers and winemakers sticking with Carménère.

In a similar mix-up, many vineyards once thought to be Cabernet Franc in Northeast Italy have proved to be Carménère. There are a few small plantings in of this variety Australia.

Carménère is used to make varietal wines and also as a component of blends, often with Cabernet Sauvignon and Merlot. The wines are typically low in acid. They have attractive savoury flavours. If the grapes are picked too early, poorer-quality wines with a marked capsicum flavour are produced.

Food choices: Think Chilean Empanadas. These are small pastries filled with meat, seafood, cheese or vegetables; and are either baked or fried. Carménère wines are light- to medium-bodied; and can be paired with poultry, pork and lamb dishes.

Chambourcin

shahm-boor-SAN
(Origin: France, Rank: 251)
Aromas and flavours: Black cherries, bubblegum, spicy, gamy.
Similar varieties: Isabella.

This variety is a French hybrid. This is a slightly misleading term and deserves an explanation. In fact, nowadays most French hybrids are banned from French vineyards.

One response to the Phylloxera plague in the late 19th century was to create new varieties by cross-breeding European grape varieties with various native American species of the Vitis genus. A more accurate term for these varieties would be American hybrids, but we are stuck with that term.

The resulting varieties are resistant to Phylloxera, and also have the virtue of being resistant to fungal diseases that afflict grape vines in humid regions.

The problem with French hybrid wines is that the wines often have unpleasant 'foxy' flavours. Some varieties are also low in acid in some areas, which means adjustments in the winemaking technique. Chambourcin usually does not have the foxy-flavour problem, and is thus the most successful of the French hybrids.

Chambourcin is grown in France, various American states, and Australia.

Chambourcin is used for dry red (alone or in blends), for rosé, as a sparkling wine, and for fortified wines. It is prized for its deeply coloured reds.

Food choices: It is difficult to generalise about foods to pair with this variety because of the range of styles. The rich reds go well with beef or barbecued kangaroo; the rosé style, perhaps with composed salads; and the fortified styles could be enjoyed with sharp vintage cheese.

Cinsaut

san-SOH
(Origin: France, Rank: 25)
Aromas and flavours: Aromatic, earthy, tar, plums, vanilla.
Similar varieties: Carignan, Pinotage, Grenache.

This is another variety whose reputation is tarnished by its ability to produce high yields of low-quality wine. It thrives in hotter regions such as the Languedoc, Corsica, and in South Africa. It is grown in Italy under the name of Ottavianello; and in Australia, it was formerly known as Blue Imperial.

It is the parent, along with Pinot Noir, of the South African variety Pinotage.

Treated well in the vineyard, Cinsaut can make good red wines, either alone or more commonly as a component of blends. It is one of the permitted varieties in Châteauneuf-du-Pape AOC, but rarely plays a prominent role.

The variety is also used to make rosé wine, and as a component of fortified port-style wines.

Food choices: The assertive spicy flavours of red wines made from Cinsaut suggest hearty stews, or perhaps mildly spiced tagines and couscous. Cinsaut is commonly made, alone or in a blend, into rosé. You could do worse than serving a salad niçoise or a ratatouille with a chilled glass of Cinsaut rosé.

Cot
— See Malbec

Dolcetto
dohl-CHET-oh
(Origin: Italy, Rank: 94)
Aromas and flavours: Black cherries, almonds, liquorice.

This variety is grown extensively in Northern Italy, especially in Piedmont, Lombardy and Liguria. There is little Dolcetto to be found elsewhere in the world, apart from several regions of Australia.

The name of this variety means "the little sweetie", but the wines are usually dry. Dolcetto wines are often bright, deeply coloured and low in tannins. Don't bother ageing these wines; they are simple and can be enjoyed within a couple of years of vintage. As well as dry reds, Dolcetto is also used for rosé.

Food choices: These wines are simple and refreshing, ideal for informal meals such as barbecues and pizza. From left field, why not try a Dolcetto with roast beetroot?

Dornfelder
Dawn-fell-der
(Origin: Germany, Rank: 84)
Aromas and flavours: This is a juicy aromatic variety with hints of cherries, blackberries and elderberries.
Similar varieties: Pinot Noir, Blaufränkisch, Cabernet Sauvignon.

Dornfelder is a relative newcomer to the scene. It was bred in Germany in the 1950s, with Pinot Noir and Blaufränkisch among its ancestors.

In the early years of this century, it had a surge of popularity in Germany and nearby Central European countries. In Germany, it is now the second most popular variety after Pinot Noir. Its ability to thrive in cooler climates has also made it a favourite of winemakers in England.

Another favourable quality of this variety is its ability to make deeply coloured wines. It was probably this characteristic that made it popular originally as a blending variety.

The wines are dark, rich and velvety, with juicy aromatics.

Food choices: Try having these with German charcuterie, such as liverwurst or smoked sausages and ham.

Durif
duh-RHIF
(Origin: France, Rank: 133, a.k.a. Petite Sirah)
Aromas and flavours: Black plums, liquorice, cherries, blackberries.
Similar varieties: Shiraz, Mavrud, Malbec.

This variety was bred in France in the 19th century as a cross between Syrah and Peloursin. It is known in Australia as Durif; and in the US, under the name Petite Sirah. It is rarely found in France these days. In Australia, Durif is best known as a classic variety from Rutherglen, but it is also grown in most warmer wine regions.

In California, a group of winemaker fans promote the variety via an organisation and website named PS I Love You.

Durif is used to make wines emphasising 'brutal power'. They wines are usually full-bodied, intensely flavoured and deeply coloured. Some are loaded with tannins, which require extended bottle ageing. Some Australian winemakers use Durif for sparkling red-wine styles.

Durif is also used as a blending partner with varieties such as Shiraz and Zinfandel.

Food choices: These are usually big wines, so try them with hearty beef and game dishes. An ideal pairing is with barbecue seared kangaroo fillet.

Gamay
ga-MAY
(Origin: France, Rank: 30, Prime name: Gamay Noir)
Aromas and flavours: Raspberries, strawberries, cherries.
Similar varieties Cabernet Franc, Blaufränkisch, Pinot Noir.

This variety is grown in many regions of France, notably in Burgundy and the Loire regions. It is highly regarded in Switzerland, where it is used to make the red wine called Dole.

Gamay is best known as the variety behind Beaujolais wine, and unfortunately Beaujolais is best known in the form of Beaujolais Nouveau. In case you missed it, Beaujolais Nouveau is released with much fanfare and marketing pizzazz on the third Thursday of November. This promotion started in the 1970s, with companies racing to be the first to deliver the new wine to Paris and other cities in a sort of precursor to television reality shows.

But Gamay deserves much more serious attention than this. Now that the Nouveau craziness is passing, the variety is increasing being used to make superb light-to medium-weight wines. Try the Beaujolais Villages rather than the Nouveau, and you will see what I mean.

Gamay is sometimes blended with Pinot Noir, but is more often used for varietal red wines and sometimes rosé wine.

Food choices: Medium-weight Gamay wines go well with charcuterie, roasted poultry or pork. If you want to pair red wine with fish, perhaps this variety will fit the bill. For something a little different, try grilled salmon steaks and Gamay.

Garnacha
— See Grenache

Graciano
grah-ee-YAH-noh
(Origin: Spain, Rank: 142)
Aromas and flavours: Spicy, aromatic, red fruits, mint.
Similar varieties: Petit Verdot, Carignan, Mourvèdre

This variety is grown in Northern Spain, especially in the Rioja and Navarre regions. In Southern France, it is grown under the name of Morrastel. In Sardinia, it is grown under the names of Bovale Sardo or Cagnulari; while in Portugal, its name is Tinta Muida. Graciano is also grown in the USA and Australia.

In Spain, Graciano is most often found in blends, typically with Tempranillo, and perhaps with some

Grenache or Cabernet Sauvignon as well. In Australia, it is used in blends, but also as a varietal wine.

Graciano is valued for its deep colour and powerful aromatics, hence its role in blends. Sometimes it lacks structure as a varietal, but more often it produces superb but underrated wines.

Food choices: Graciano wines can be enjoyed with something Spanish, maybe rabbit paella, or a stew of chorizo with beans or lentils. The soft flavours and middle weight of these wines are also great with roast lamb or chicken.

Grenache
gren-AHSH
(Origin: Spain, Rank: 7, Prime name: Granacha)
Aromas and flavours: Raspberries, pepper, spices, cherries.
Similar varieties: Zinfandel, Carignan, Barbera.

Its Spanish origin suggests that Garnacha is probably the more correct name. But in the anglophone world, Grenache is the most commonly used name. It is grown in most warm to hot regions of the world, although it is only of minor importance in South America and South Africa.

In France, Grenache is used extensively throughout the South. It is a major component of the Châteauneuf-du-Pape DOCG.

WHAT VARIETAL IS THAT?

Grenache is most commonly blended, as in the case of Châteauneuf-du-Pape, but also in many other appellations of Southern France.

In Spain, Grenache makes varietal wines; and it is also used in blends with Tempranillo or, in the case of Priorat in Catalonia, with Carignan. On the the Italian island of Sardinia, this variety makes red wines under the name of Cannonau.

Considerable amounts are grown in California and, more recently, in Washington State.

In the 1980s, Grenache was regarded as an inferior variety and was subject to an Australian Government-sponsored vine pull scheme. Fortunately, some old Grenache vineyards survived, and the variety is now more widely appreciated.

There are some Australian varietal Grenache wines but more often it plays the leading role blended red wines. For example Grenache is often often in GSM blends, along with Shiraz and Mourvèdre.

The quality of Grenache wines varies considerably. If allowed to overcrop, the wines are thin, pale and uninspiring. The best wines form this variety are produced from hard-pruned old vines grown in hot unirrigated conditions.

Grenache is often used alone or in blends to make rosé wines. Some of the best are from Provence, and the Spanish region of Navarre.

There are Gris and Blanc versions of the variety, both of which are locally important in parts of Southern France and Spain.

Food choices: The structure and length of Grenache red wines is ideal for Moroccan-spiced dishes such as lamb and quince tagine. Grenache rosé wines can be enjoyed with Provençal style appetisers like tapenade or stuffed vegetables such as tomatoes or courgettes.

Lagrein
lah-GRINE
(Origin: Italy, Rank: 315)
Aromas and flavours: Plums, dark chocolate, berries, herbs, spices.
Similar varieties: Shiraz, Cabernet Sauvignon.

Lagrein is grown mainly in Northeastern Italy, in particular, the region of Trentino-Alto Adige, from whence it originated. Varietal red wines are made and it is also blended with the local varieties.

There is some of this variety grown in California and Australia.

The reds made from Lagrein are typically fruity, deeply coloured and have moderate tannins. Lagrein is also often made into rosé styles.

Food choices: The fuller-bodied styles would be good with grilled pork and fennel sausages. Lighter styles or Lagrein rosata could be enjoyed with antipasto or a simple platter of prosciutto.

Lambrusco
Lam-BROO-sko
(Origin: Italy, Rank: 170*)
Aromas and flavours: Raspberries, strawberries. Dry, full-bodied examples are rich and earthy.
Similar varieties: Brachetto.

The word 'Lambrusco' is unfortunately associated with the style of wine more than with the grape varieties that use the name. Lambrusco, for most wine lovers, is the extremely cheap, pallid, low-acid, low-alcohol, moderately or even excessively sweet, and sometimes fizzy drink. It ticks all of the boxes of what we are trained to disdain.

But there is more to Lambrusco than that. There are in fact many distinct varieties of Lambrusco and Lambrusca in the Italian regions of Emilia-Romagna and Piedmont. They are used to make a variety of wine styles, from the popular easy-drinking, semi-sweet versions to quite dense and full-bodied dry reds.

The range of styles made from these varieties demonstrates a major fault in the practice of varietal labelling. Two wines can be as far apart as you could imagine, but still be labelled 'Lambrusco'.

Lambrusco varieties are mainly confined to Italy, but there are tiny amounts in Australia and Argentina.

One particular variety, Lambrusco Maestri, stands out as being capable of making full-bodied red wines.

Food choices: The lighter styles are ideal for antipasto or many typical Italian dishes. You could try them with fruit-based desserts. The full-bodied versions are probably best consumed along with a grilled T-bone steak.

Malbec
MAHL-beck
(Origin: France, Rank: 21, Prime name: Cot)
Aromas and flavours: Black cherries, chocolate, plums, violets, spices.
Similar varieties: Cabernet Sauvignon, Shiraz.

Malbec originated in the Cahors region of Southwestern France, where it is called Cot. Nobody else calls it that, but you could argue that Cot is the correct name.

It is a minor component of some Bordeaux blends, and it is used in other French regions as a blending component. But its best French expression is in the so-called black wines of Cahors. These are usually varietal Malbec, but sometimes contain some Tannat. Cahors wines are typically soft, aromatic, and of course, deeply coloured.

Most famously, Malbec is the leading red wine variety of Argentina, where it makes everything from everyday drinking wines through to the highest-quality, age-worthy reds. It is used in many other parts of the world, either as blending material or increasingly as a straight varietal.

Malbec is valued for its deep colour and firm tannins. Sometimes, these are too prominent for some palates. Clonal selection, careful winemaking, and blending minor amounts of other varieties is now used to make more approachable wines.

Food choices: For the fuller, more rustic Argentine styles of Malbec, you could consider the typical Argentinian Asado — a heroic mixture of meats, sausages and offal grilled over charcoal. If you are not entertaining a crowd, a simple barbecue will suffice.

More subtle styles of Malbec, like the Cahors versions, are more suited to slow-cooked meat-based casseroles or roasted game meats.

Mataro
— See Mourvèdre

Mazuella
— See Carignan

RED WINE VARIETIES

Mencia
men-THEE-ah
(Origin Spain, Rank 65)
Aromas and flavours: Blackberries, cherries, herbs, spices, vanilla.
Similar varieties: Graciano, Pinot Noir, Gamay, Cabernet Franc.

Mencia is a newly emerging variety from Northwest Spain and Portugal. It is grown in the DO regions of Bierzo, Ribiera Sacra and Valdeorras in Spain; and in the Dao region of Portugal, where it is known as Jaen.

Mencia has only recently attracted the attention of the wine world, and it has the potential to become a superstar variety. One problem is that this variety was discovered by UK wine journalists and supermarket buyers, causing a surge in demand. The demand was met by lower-quality wines of dubious provenance, so cheaper wines sold as Mencia can be disappointing.

The wines made from Mencia are rich and flavoursome, but the tannins are not overwhelming. The middle palate delivers a kaleidoscope of fruit flavours, but the weight of the wine is not usually overpowering.

A few Australian winemakers are now producing Mencia wine.

Food choices: This soft and rich wine would be good with grilled octopus, or with roast kid.

Merlot
mer-LOH
(Origin: France, Rank: 2)
Aromas and flavours: Plums, black cherries, prunes.
Similar varieties: Carménère.

This is a much maligned variety, and was the subject of a notorious derogatory quote in a Hollywood movie. However, let the facts speak for themselves. It is grown throughout the wine world, except in the coolest climates; it is the most commonly planted variety in France; and globally, it is second only to Cabernet Sauvignon in area planted.

Merlot's virtues and successes have become its enemies. As an early-ripening variety, it can be grown in cooler areas. It performs well in the vineyard; and typically produces fresh, soft wines with a sweet middle palate and no nasty tannins. The resulting easy-drinking wines are often dismissed by critics as lacking a distinctive character, and wine writers often find it difficult to come up with arresting descriptors.

Although a large proportion of Merlot grapes find their way into blends, mostly with Cabernet Sauvignon, there are plenty of varietal examples around. At the top end are the varietal Merlots from the Pomerol region of Bordeaux. Château Pétrus from Pomerol is one of the most expensive wines in the world. But most people experience Merlot in the form of wines in the low-to-middle price ranges.

Merlot is grown throughout the wine world, most often in blends with Cabernet Sauvignon. In blends, it adds softness to otherwise harsh wines.

Food choices: Merlot is most often made into easy-drinking wines with soft tannins, so you can keep the food simple as well. It's ideal with charcuterie, or with simple meat dishes or coq au vin.

Monastrell
— See Mourvèdre

Montepulciano
MOHN-teh-pool-CHAH-noh
(Origin: Italy, Rank: 27)
Aromas and flavours: Plums, pepper, spices, cherries, violets.
Similar varieties: Sangiovese, Graciano.

There is a minor confusion to be cleared up about this name. The name Montepulciano refers to a town near Sienna in Tuscany, the Vino Nobile di Montepulciano DOCG area around that town, as well as the red wine grape variety. Vino Nobile di Montepulciano is, in fact, made from Sangiovese.

The Montepulciano grape is grown throughout Central Italy, most famously as Montepulciano d'Abruzzo. Montepulciano is the second most widely planted red wine grape in Italy but strangely, the wines are not highly regarded.

It is not an important variety outside Italy; although in recent years, some stunning, majestic wines have been made with Montepulciano in South Australia.

Wines made from this wine are deeply coloured and can be quite tannic. These characteristics mean that Montepulciano is often blended in Italy, and perhaps explain why the variety gets so little attention in Italy.

Food choices: For lighter styles, you could pair them with tomato-based pasta sauces, or antipasto. More robust examples, especially those from South Australia, call for meatier dishes.

Mourvèdre
moor-VEDH-ruh
(Origin: Spain, Rank: 14, Prime name: Monastrell)
Aromas and flavours: Blackberries, cherries, spices, leather, herbs.
Similar varieties: Graciano, Zinfandel.

The anglophone world tends to use the French name Mourvèdre for this variety, but the Spanish name Monastrell is more correct in that it originated in Spain. There is a much greater area planted in Spain than in France. In California and Australia, it was long called Mataro. There was a trend of calling it Mourvèdre from the 1990s; but mercifully, in Australia at least, more winemakers are reverting to the name Mataro.

This variety's main use is as blending material, often with Grenache and Syrah to make red wines or rosé.

The highly regarded Bandol from Provence is a Mourvèdre-dominant blend. In Australia, Mourvèdre is most often found in GSM blends, with Grenache and Shiraz making up the rest of the acronym.

There are a few varietal wines made from this variety, but care needs to be taken by the winemaker to control its tendency to produce high alcohols and tannins.

Food choices: Fuller-bodied Mourvèdre wines call for meaty dishes, either grilled or stewed. They will also stand up to moderately spicy dishes. Softer styles and blends can go with poultry, veal or mushroom-based dishes. When pairing Mourvèdre rosé wines with food, remember its Mediterranean origin and serve them with eggplant or zucchini dishes, or perhaps with tapenade.

Nebbiolo
neb-BYOH-loh
(Origin: Italy, Rank: 99, Aussie producers 150+)
Aromas and flavours: Tar, roses, violets, cherries, earthy, smoky.
Similar varieties: Aglianico, Pinot Noir.

This is the premium wine variety of Italy, and its stronghold is the region of Piedmont, in the foothills of the Alps. Two Piedmontese villages, separated by just a few kilometres, give their names to the Barolo DOCG and Barbaresco DOCG. These are widely held as the best examples, but there are many other vineyards throughout Piedmont and the neighbouring regions of Valle d'Aosta and Lombardy.

WHAT VARIETAL IS THAT?

Some vineyards have a small proportion of the white variety Arneis interplanted, and the blend is co-fermented in a similar way to Shiraz Viognier.

This is not a variety for novices: not in the vineyard, not in the winery, and not in the glass.

Nebbiolo is difficult to grow successfully outside its home territory, but hardy souls in Argentina, Australia, Chile, Mexico and the United States have persisted to establish vineyards and to make some excellent wines.

Wines made from Nebbiolo are typically brownish, even when young. They also have assertive tannins and, in some cases, they need extended ageing.

The trials and tribulations in making Nebbiolo are often rewarded by sensational wines full of haunting flavours and aromas.

Food choices: The earthiness of Nebbiolo makes it ideal for dishes with all types of mushrooms, truffles, and wild boar. Meat-based sauces such as a ragu made with duck meat are also good ways to appreciate these wines. The classic Piedmontese dish is brasato al barolo — beef braised in Barolo wine.

Negroamaro

NEH-groh-uh-MAHR-oh
(Origin: Italy, Rank: 60)
Aromas and flavours: Blackberries, pepper, herbs.
Similar varieties: Primitivo.

The name is sometimes spelt as Negro Amaro. It means something like "black bitter", although there is a theory that it could mean "black black".

It grows in the warm regions of Puglia, Basilicata and Campania in South Italy. There are only small amounts grown outside Italy, but some innovative winemakers in California and Australia are starting to make Negroamaro wines.

The red wines made from this variety are often full-bodied and high in alcohol. In the past, much of the production was surreptitiously shipped north in bulk to be blended with other Italian red wine varieties. In Puglia, Negroamaro is often blended with lesser amounts of other red wine varieties such as Malvasia Nera, Montepulciano, and Sangiovese.

One of the most successful expressions of this variety is Salice Salentino DOC, which has a minimum of 80% Negroamaro and up to 20% of Malvasia Nera.

Negroamaro is also used to make still rosado wine, and also pink sparkling wine.

Food choices: The robust flavours of Negroamaro can be highlighted by orecchiette con cime di rapa, ear-shaped pasta with bitter greens, which is one of the classic dishes of Puglia. Other pasta dishes with meat-based sauces are also suitable.

Nero d'Avola

NEH-roh DAH-voh-jah
(Origin: Italy, Rank: 60)
Aromas and flavours: Blackberries, plums, earth, violets, spices.
Similar varieties: Some people say Shiraz, but I can't see the similarity.

The name of the variety derives from the town of Avola in Southeast Sicily, although the nickname "Black Devil" is popular in some circles. This variety is also called Calabrese, even though very little is grown on mainland Italy. Several other Italian varieties are also called Calabrese, so there is plenty of confusion, but that's Italian wine.

Nero d'Avola is by far the most extensively grown variety in Sicily. Until recently, very little was grown outside Italy.

That will change as the variety is attracting plenty of attention in Australia, where its ability to thrive in hot climates and still produce wines with delicious flavours and sufficient acidity is seen as a virtue. In fact, the trophies for the Best Wine of Show at the Australian Alternative Varieties Wine Show in 2016 and 2017 were awarded to Nero d'Avola wines from the Coriole and Hither & Yon wineries, respectively.

This variety makes deeply coloured red wines which can be aged, as well as lighter-bodied wines for everyday drinking. Nero is most often used as a varietal, but blends with other Italian and international varieties are also fairly common. Nero also makes excellent rosado.

Food choices: The generally lighter-bodied wines make this variety ideal for summer drinking with lighter Mediterranean dishes. Pasta Norma is a classic Sicilian dish with an aubergine and tomato-based sauce. Another Sicilian favourite is Arancini, which would be suitably accompanied by Nero d'Avola rosé.

Petit Verdot
peh-TEE vair-DOH
(Origin: France, Rank: 90)
Aromas and flavours: Violets, blackberries, plums, spices.
Similar varieties: Fer, Gros Verdot.

This is a minor Bordeaux variety which is used mainly for blending with the more favoured varieties of Cabernet Sauvignon, Merlot and Cabernet Franc. It adds deep colour, firm acidity, flavours and tannins to blends. It ripens later than other Bordeaux varieties in that region; and in cooler years, it doesn't ripen at all. This gives meaning to its name: the little green one.

Petit Verdot is valued for adding colour and flavour to blends. It is often a minor component of some of the higher-priced Bordeaux wines.

Outside France, it is grown in Spain, Portugal and California, mostly for use in so-called Bordeaux blends, but there are plenty of varietal examples as well.

Around the turn of the 21st century, Petit Verdot became popular in warmer Australian regions for making varietal wines. Many Australian growers and winemakers use it as an alternative to Shiraz, its late-ripening trait seen as a virtue in warmer areas.

Food choices: As a varietal, the firm tannins in the wine suggest you should enjoy it with red meat dishes, perhaps steak sandwiches or a barbecued duck breast.

Petite Sirah
— See Durif

Pinot Meunier
pee-noh Moon-YAY
(Origin: France, Rank: 63)
Aromas and flavours: Similar to Pinot Noir, but more fragrant and fruitier. Sometimes has citrus or candied-fruit flavours.
Similar varieties: Pinot Noir, Gamay.

This variety is genetically identical to Pinot Noir, except for a few mutant genes. So strictly speaking, it is a clone of Pinot Noir, as are Pinot Gris/Grigio and Pinot Blanc.

RED WINE VARIETIES

However, these clones are all sufficiently different in the vineyard and in the winery that they are generally regarded as being distinct varieties.

The most striking difference between Meunier and Noir in the vineyard is that the underside of the leaves of Meunier appear white, as though they have been dusted with flour. This gives rise to the name Meunier, which means miller, and to a common synonym, 'Miller's Burgundy'. In fact, the underside of the leaf is covered with a layer of fine hairs.

The major use of this variety is for making sparkling wines. Along with Pinot Noir and Chardonnay, Pinot Meunier makes up the trilogy of varieties in Champagne. These same three are grown together in many other parts of the world where winemakers seek to emulate the blend of varieties in Champagne.

This variety is also used to make dry red wines, especially in Australia. Varietal Pinot Meunier wines tend to be light-bodied but quite flavourful. They tend to be fruitier than Pinot Noir. These are relatively uncommon, but are well worth seeking out.

Food choices: The soft flavours of this wine are well suited to such dishes as rack of lamb or grilled chicken livers.

Pinot Noir
(Origin: France, Rank: 10)

Aromas and flavours: It is hard to generalise about the precise aromas. In a good Pinot Noir, there are hints of all sorts of fruits — berries, cherries, plums with floral backgrounds. Sometimes, there are spicy overtones. More complex flavours evolve with age in the fuller-bodied wines.

Similar varieties: Pinot Meunier, Gamay.

The finest, and most expensive, expressions of this variety are found in the red wines of Burgundy. At the top end, these are some of the best wines in the world. The quality of the wine seems to be highly dependent on the precise microclimate of the vineyards. Only tiny amounts are made, and scarcity conspires with quality to elevate the prices to dizzying levels.

Winemakers around the world have planted Pinot Noir in an effort to produce Burgundy-style wines. In warmer areas, this aim has proved impossible. In other areas, selecting the right clones and getting the viticulture right have been challenging. In recent decades, the quality of non-Burgundian Pinot Noir has improved markedly.

As mentioned earlier, Pinot Noir is also one of the favoured trinity to make Champagne. The other varieties are its twin sister Pinot Meunier and Chardonnay. The juice of the red grapes is extracted quickly so that only the tiniest amount of colour, if any, gets into the fermenting juice.

Again, sparkling winemakers around the world seek to emulate Champagne by using the same varieties, but as Champagne is a geographic name, they need to call the wine something else.

Food choices: The tannins and earthiness of Pinot Noir can match it with a variety of foods. Try it with chicken liver pate, grilled lamb kidneys, mushrooms or truffles. Why not marry the classic Chinese dish of Peking duck with the classic French wine of Burgundy?

Pinotage
pee-noh-TAHJ
(Origin: South Africa, Rank: 93)
Aromas and flavours: Smokey, gamey, blackberries, burnt rubber.
Similar varieties: Zinfandel, Shiraz, full-bodied Pinot Noir.

Pinotage was bred in South Africa during the 1920s as a crossing of Cinsaut and Pinot Noir. In South Africa at that time, Cinsaut was known as Hermitage in South Africa, so the name naturally evolved from the names of its parents. As a side note, the name Hermitage was also used as a synonym for the varieties Shiraz and Marsanne, probably because all three are grown in the Hermitage AOC region of the Rhone Valley.

This variety is grown extensively in South Africa. There are small amounts in California and New Zealand, and more recently in Australia.

Pinotage is a controversial variety. As a high-yielding variety, it gained its reputation in South Africa from cheap wine. It was often used to make wines with odd and sometimes unpleasant flavours. These faults were commonly covered up by maturing the wine in charred oak barrels, giving the consumer the illusion she was drinking wine from a well-used but unwashed ashtray.

More recently, careful winemaking has produced wines which are much more acceptable to mainstream tastes, but still have the distinctive edgy, gamy flavours. Pinotage is used to make rosé and fortified styles; and is also commonly blended with other varieties such as Cabernet Sauvignon, Shiraz and Merlot.

Food choices: Lighter styles can be paired with milder Indian food. More robust styles are ideal with meaty dishes and sharp cheeses. Strongly flavoured Boerewors sausages are a South African barbecue favourite to try with these rustic wines. If you are addicted to kale, the new wonder food, then this variety might be the ideal match for you.

Plavac Mali
plah-vahtz mahlee
(Origin: Croatia, Rank: 205)
Aromas and flavours: Blackberries, cherries, pepper and spices.
Similar varieties: Zinfandel.

This is the most widely planted, and highly regarded red wine variety of Croatia. There is virtually none grown outside Croatia, but don't be surprised if it doesn't crop up elsewhere in the near future.

For many years, there was controversy about its true identity, with many producers claiming that it was really Zinfandel. It would have been quite a commercial advantage to exporters if they could label their wines as Zinfandel in the US market. Eventually, DNA analysis has shown that Plavac Mali is in fact a separate variety, with one parent being Zinfandel and the other, an obscure Croatian variety called Dobricic.

The wines from this variety are typically darkly coloured, and high in tannins and acid. It is widely planted, and the quality of the wines fills the full gamut of rough and rustic through to some of the most elegant red wines of Croatia. The name Plavac refers to the bluish tint of the grapes.

Food choices: A couple of Croatian favourites — grilled cevapcici sausages, red peppers stuffed with rice and minced lamb.

Primitivo
— See Zinfandel

Ruby Cabernet
ROO-be ka-ber-NAY
(Origin: USA, Rank: 101)
Aromas and flavours: Fruity tomatoes.

This variety originated in the 1930s as a cross between Cabernet Sauvignon and Carignan. The aim was to breed a variety with some of the flavours of Cabernet, but with the higher yields and heat tolerance of Carignan.

Of all of the artificial cross-bred varieties, this one is among the most successful. It is grown in California and other states, as well as Australia and South Africa. It thrives in hot irrigated regions, but doesn't produce wines of any great distinction.

It is used as a varietal, but more commonly it is blended to bulk out other everyday red wines.

Food choices: Pair it with Chinese-style steak and black bean sauce, Caribbean foods, and mildly spicy dishes.

Sagrantino
sah-grahn-TEE-noh
(Origin: Italy, Rank: 267)
Aromas and flavours: Cherries, vanilla, plums, blackberries, mulberries, chocolate.
Similar varieties: Tempranillo, Mencia.

This variety is the specialty of the region around Montefalco in Umbria. It was formerly used to make sweet and sacramental wines. The name is believed to derive from the Italian word for sacred. Since the 1960s, Sagrantino is much more famous for its deeply coloured, richly flavoured dry red wines. These darkly brooding wines tend to be high in tannins and age-worthy. Sagrantino is most often used as a varietal, but it is also sometimes blended with Sangiovese.

There are also some passito-style wines made with Sagrantino which are sweeter and richer.

The revival and outstanding success of the variety in Umbria has prompted planting in other Italian regions, notably Tuscany and Sicily. Sagrantino is also grown in California; and more recently, some Australian wineries have made some stunning wines with it.

Food Choices: These rich wines can be enjoyed with charcuterie, especially Noriciera — the sausages and cured products of wild boar, which are the specialty of the town of Norcia in Umbria.

Sangiovese
SAN-joh-VAY-zay
(Origin: Italy, Rank: 13)
Aromas and flavours: Plums, cherries, blackberries, herbs, tomatoes, spices.
Similar varieties: Nero d'Avola, Montepulciano.

Sangiovese is the most commonly grown red wine variety in Italy. There are many clones of this variety, and some argue that there are distinct varieties grown under the name.

WHAT VARIETAL IS THAT?

It is best known as the variety behind Chianti, Tuscany's flagship wine. In fact, this variety is grown throughout Central and Southern Italy to make varietal wines or as a component of blends.

Sangiovese is the only variety permitted in the famous wines from Brunello di Montalcino, which are regarded as among Italy's best. They're made from a strain of Sangiovese Grosso called Brunello ("little dark one"), so named for the brown hue of its skin. Although these wines are grown and made in Tuscany, they are big, deep-coloured, and powerful, with enough tannins and structure to warrant considerable cellaring.

Sangiovese is often used to make straight varietal wines; but blends are also common, either with other Italian varieties such as Canaiolo Nera and Mammolo, or with the so-called international varieties. In the latter case, Sangiovese is blended with one or more of Cabernet Sauvignon, Merlot, Cabernet Franc or Syrah to make the so-called Super Tuscan wines.

Outside Italy, Sangiovese has a minor presence in many wine-growing countries. On the French island of Corsica, under the name of Neilluccio, Sangiovese is the main red wine variety. Over the past few decades, this variety has been embraced in Australia as one of the pioneers of the alternative varieties.

Food choices: The everyday drinking types are ideal accompaniments to pizza and tomato-based pasta sauces. More serious versions call for meaty dishes such as Bistecca alla Fiorentina — T-bone steak grilled over charcoal.

Sankt Laurent
Saint Laur-ent
(Origin: Austria, Rank: 147)
Aromas and flavours: Sour cherries, spicy.
Similar varieties: Pinot Noir.

This is a red wine variety most commonly associated with Austria, where it is becoming increasingly popular. It is named after the patron saint of chefs.

It is also increasing used in Germany. It is grown in several other Central European countries.
There is now a growing interest in the variety in several New World countries, including Australia.

The variety produces wines which are velvety and deeply coloured (hence, the German synonym Schwarzer, or black).

Food choices: You can match the spiciness of these wines with some Middle European favourites such as bratwurst sausages with sauerkraut, or sauerbraten — pickled marinated beef with juniper berries, cloves and nutmeg.

Saperavi

sa-per-AH-vee
(Origin: Georgia, Rank: 82)
Aromas and flavours: Violets, Blackberries.
Similar varieties: Xinmavro.

Saperavi is a red wine grape variety that is a native of Georgia in the former Soviet Union.
It was the most popular grape variety planted in many of the wine-producing republics. As you might expect, this variety is well-adapted to continental climates with extreme heat in summer and cold in winter, but it can be grown successfully in maritime climates.

The characteristic of the grapes of this exciting variety are the dark pink flesh and very dark skins; hence, wines made from this variety are deeply coloured. In fact, the name of the variety means 'dyer' in the Georgian language. Another notable characteristic of wines made from this variety is the high acid levels, which makes it suitable for blending.

Saperavi is also used to make semi-sweet wines and port-style fortified wines.

Food choices: Saperavi can be enjoyed with smoked meats, or hearty winter stews.

RED WINE VARIETIES

Shiraz
SHE-rahz
(Origin: France, Rank: 6, Prime name: Syrah)
Aromas and flavours: Blackberries, pepper, herbs, spices.
Similar varieties: Durif (a.k.a. Petite Sirah), Monduese.

This variety almost certainly originated the Northern Rhone region of France. Some believe that it is from the ancient Persian city of Shiraz because of the shared name. However, historical and DNA evidence makes this hypothesis extremely unlikely; and of course, the original name is Syrah, not Shiraz.

Shiraz is most often associated with Australia, where it is the most commonly grown variety. There is a larger area grown in France. Outside these two countries, Shiraz became popular during the later decades of the 20th century, and is now grown in most mild to warm wine regions.

The versatility of this variety is that it will thrive in most warm climates and can make a variety of styles, from the oceans of bulk wine from the irrigated regions to the heavily concentrated wines from old vines in the traditional regions.

Shiraz is often blended with other varieties, for example, with Grenache and Mourvèdre in the classic GSM blends of South Australia; or with Cabernet Sauvignon and Malbec.

The early 21st century saw a wave of popularity for Shiraz Viognier, not a blend but the result of co-fermentation of Shiraz with a small amount of the white variety. These wines are more brightly coloured and have a slightly different flavour profile.

The styles of Shiraz and Shiraz-dominated wines vary greatly. When wine writer Robert Parker was at the peak of his influence, big-bodied, high-alcohol wines were in abundance. Now, slightly lighter styles with a less overbearing oak influence are making a comeback.

Shiraz is also used to make fortified, port-style wines.

Food choices: Shiraz is suitable for most meaty dishes, from simple barbeques to rich gamy meat dishes. Braised lamb shanks is a popular pairing.

Syrah
— See Shiraz

Tannat
tah-NOH
(Origin: France, Rank: 100)
Aromas and flavours: Blackberries, blackcurrants, black plums, vanilla, spices.
Similar varieties: Zinfandel, Malbec, Durif.

Tannat is a robust red wine variety from Southwest France. It is the main variety of the Madiran AOC, where it makes deeply coloured tannic wines, sometimes moderated by blending with Cabernet Franc or Cabernet

Sauvignon. Tannat also very popular in Uruguay, where it was introduced by immigrants from the Basque regions of Spain and France.

Tannat wines typically require extended ageing, although in more recent times, easy-drinking lighter styles have been made using modified winemaking techniques.

Food choices: The high level of acidity and tannins in these wines call for robust foods: cassoulet, duck confit, rich game birds, potatoes roasted in goose fat, oxtail stew. Beef and Tannat are both national obsessions in Uruguay. Try a slow barbecued beef rib eye steak with a glass or two to find out why.

Tempranillo
temp-rah-NEE-yoh
(Origin: Spain, Rank: 4)
Aromas and flavours: Ripe cherries, black olive, plums, fennel, oregano, rosemary.
Similar varieties: Pinot Noir, Cabernet Sauvignon, Sangiovese.

This variety has undergone the most spectacular increase in area vines since the turn of the millennium, overwhelming Spain, which has about 90% of the world's plantings. There are considerable plantings also in Portugal (under several names, including Aragonês and Tinta Roriz), France, Argentina, Uruguay, United States and Australia.

In Spain, Tempranillo grows mainly on the 'unrainy' plain where the terroir is decidedly continental.
The most famous region in Spain for this variety is Rioja, but it is also well-known for its role in the Ribera del Duero and Toro regions. It plays a role in most other Spanish regions as well.
Tempranillo wines are often classed according to their age and oak treatment. Joven styles are unoaked and crafted to be consumed young. Crianza, Reserva and Gran Reserva classes must spend increasing time in oak, and are bottle-aged for defined periods before being sold.

In Portugal, Tempranillo, under several aliases, is important for making Port wines and also dry reds in several regions.

One of the characteristics of good Tempranillo wines is that they have a good fruity middle palate, but with a firm finish.

Tempranillo is often made into a varietal wine, but it is also frequently blended with one or more other varieties such as Grenache, Graciano, Cabernet Sauvignon and Merlot.

Tempranillo also makes exceptional rosé-style wines, for example, from the Northern Spanish region of Navarre.

Food choices: The Spanish origin of this variety suggests roast suckling lamb, jamon (the Spanish answer to prosciutto), and rustic Spanish stews including perhaps chorizo and beans.

Touriga Nacional
too-REE-gah nah-see-yoo-NAHL
(Origin: Portugal, Rank: 67)
Aromas and flavours: Cherries, black pepper, blackberries, violets, spices.
Similar varieties: Touriga Franca, Zinfandel.

There are three varieties sharing the Touriga name: Touriga Nacional (the parent); and Touriga Franca and Touriga Femea. There's only a tiny amount of Femea grown. Touriga Franca is more widely planted than Touriga Nacional in Portugal, but is regarded as producing lesser quality wines.

Touriga Nacional is the most highly regarded of the Port varieties in the Douro. There are also significant plantings in other regions of Portugal, in the Priorat region of Catalonia, in California, South Africa and Australia. In Australia, the variety is often simply referred to as Touriga; there is little or no Touriga Franca in Australia.

This red wine variety was most commonly used in blends to make Port wine, where it is valued for adding flavour and aroma to the blend. In more recent times, Touriga is increasingly used alone or blended to make dry red wines.

Food choices: Touriga wines can be lush and robust, and hence are well suited to grilled or smoked meat dishes, or perhaps with some field mushrooms cooked with garlic.

Tribidrag (a.k.a. Primitivo, Zinfandel)
— See Zinfandel

Trousseau
(Origin: France, Rank: 136)
Aromas and flavours: Strawberries, raspberries, herbs.
Similar varieties: Pinot Noir, Castelao

This variety originated in the Jura Region of Eastern France. It is used in that region to make dry red wines. Trousseau is valued in the Jura for contributing acidity and structure to red wine blends.

This variety is used for Port, dry red table wines and rosé under the name of Bastardo in Portugal and Australia. In Galicia, Northwest Spain, it is grown under the name Merenzao. There is another minor unrelated variety called Bastardo Tinto.

Bastardo is not known for producing good varietal wines, but plays a part in some dry red blends. However, it is sometimes used to make excellent rosé-style wines.

Food choices: For the Port or port-style wines, pair with sharp or pungent cheeses, pecan pie or nuts. As a rosé, you can enjoy it as an aperitif or with an antipasto assortment.

RED WINE VARIETIES

Xinomavro
ksee-NOH-mah-vroh
(Origin: Greece, Rank: 184)
Aromas and flavours: Cherries, prunes, plums, roses, chocolate, pepper, spices.
Similar varieties: Nebbiolo, Barbera.

This is the second most planted red variety in Greece, after Agiorgitiko. The Naousa appellation is the most highly regarded expression of Xinomavro. In that region, it must be 100% of the variety; but in other Greek regions, it is blended, either with other local varieties or with something like Merlot or Shiraz.

Xinomavro wines are best aged for a few years to tone down their high levels of tannins and acidity. These characteristics, along with the light colours, prompt many commentators to draw comparisons with Nebbiolo. This variety is also used to make rosé-style wines; and in some cooler areas of Greece, it is a base for sparkling wines and even dry whites.

The Xinomavro variety is not grown to any extent outside of Greece. But the quality of some of the wines produced from it means that sooner or later, it will be taken up somewhere in a New World wine region.

Food choices: The acidity of the Xinomavro is an excellent foil for Aegean favourites like grilled meats, moussaka, calamari, octopus and shellfish.

Zinfandel (a.k.a. Primitivo, Tribidrag)
ZIN-fun-dell
(Origin: Croatia, Rank: 29)
Aromas and flavours: Plums, blackberries, pepper, blueberries, cranberries, liquorice.
Similar varieties: Plavac Mali.

The Zinfandel wine variety was the subject of a long-run discussion about its true identity. For years, Italian winemakers claimed that the Puglian variety Primitivo was in fact the same, and that they should be able to label their wines for export to the US accordingly. The Californian Zinfandel producers saw a massive commercial downside to this, and the two sides battled it out over a couple of decades. The second front on this trade war was that Croatian makers of Plavac Mali claimed that their wine was also entitled to be called Zinfandel as well.

The old way of identifying varieties relied on comparing a whole range of characteristics of the vines and the grapes. This method was very accurate, but not precise in showing that they were the same variety. The tiny amount of scientific doubt provided ammunition for adherents of the contrary view. Commercial interests can be resistant to inconvenient scientific evidence.

Since the late 1990s, DNA analysis has been used to sort out the identity and parentage of varieties. It has shown that the two varieties Zinfandel and Primitivo are indeed identical. Plavac Mali is a distinct variety whose parent is Zinfandel.

Zinfandel is known for making robust red wines. The individual grapes within each bunch ripen at different rates. This is a contributing factor in the distinctive flavour profile.

In California, its reputation was somewhat tainted by its ability to produce large quantities of jug wine; and for its use (misuse?) in producing 'White Zin', a sickly sweet rosé style.

In Puglia, Italy's heel, this variety is grown under the name of Primitivo. It is making a revival there either as a varietal wine or blended with other local varieties. It is also becoming more popular in Croatia under its local names Crljenak Kaštelanski or Tribidrag.

Food choices: Zinfandel wines are typically robust and call for well flavoured foods such as American-style beef spare ribs, game meats such as BBQ kangaroo, chilli con carne, Italian fennel sausages.

Zweigelt
TSVY-gelt
(Origin: Austria, Rank: 72)
Aromas and flavours: Cherries, plums, blackberries, cinnamon.
Similar varieties: Blaufränkisch.

This variety was bred in Austria as a cross of Blaufränkisch and Sankt Laurent. Zweigelt is now the most widely grown red wine variety in Austria; and each year, more is being planted.

It is also grown in neighbouring Central European countries, and also in the UK. The popularity of the variety is due to is high and reliable yields in cool climates.

Zweigelt is most commonly used to make unoaked, lighter-style dry reds intended for consuming while young. Fuller-bodied wines aged in oak are also made.

Food choices: The lighter-style reds are ideally suited to a charcuterie platter. Heavier Zweigelt wines can be enjoyed with dishes such as smoked hock.

Appendix

Varieties by Country and Region

Every wine country has its few favourite varieties. In Old World countries, these varieties have originated within the region and have been cultivated to be well suited to the local terroir. In this chapter, we look at the main varieties cultivated in some of the most important wine-producing countries. The varieties listed are those dominating by area planted, but I have included varieties that are otherwise noteworthy for each region.

Much of the information in this chapter is based on the book Which Winegrape Varieties are Grown Where? by Kym Anderson. The data in this publication are from about 2010; some changes have occurred since then, most notably in China, where huge new vineyards, mostly of Cabernet Sauvignon, have been planted.

APPENDIX

It makes little sense to treat France and Italy as one wine entity, so I have included a breakdown of the various regions in those two countries at the end of this chapter.

The varieties described in the main chapters of the book are indicated in **boldface.**

Argentina
The main white wines are made from **Torrontés** and Pedro Giménez (a variety different from Pedro Ximénez). Red varieties are dominated by **Malbec**, Douce Noire and Creole Grande. There is also a pink-skinned variety called Cereza (Spanish for Cherry), which is mainly used for white wine.

Australia
Shiraz, **Cabernet Sauvignon**, **Merlot** and **Chardonnay** dominate plantings in Australia; although since the turn of this century, many other varieties such as **Pinot Gris**, **Sangiovese** and **Tempranillo** have been growing in popularity.

Austria
Zweigelt and **Blaufränkisch** dominate the red wine scene here. **Grüner Veltliner** is by far the most popular white wine variety. There are also some vineyards of Grasevina, **Müller-Thurgau** and **Pinot Blanc**.

Brazil
Most of this country is too hot and humid for viticulture; but there are considerable plantings of the Isabella, Bordo and Concord red varieties and Niagara white

wine variety. All of these varieties are hybrids with non-vinifera heritage.

Bulgaria
Formerly a major supplier of cheap plonk to the Soviet Union, Bulgaria is reemerging as a maker of fine wines. The main native red varieties are Pamid, Shiroka Malnishka and Mavrud. White wines are made from Misket Chevran, Muscat Ottonel and **Rkatsiteli**.

Canada
The winter-hardy Vidal Blanc shades out **Chardonnay** as the major white wine variety. Riesling is grown for ice wine, and **Pinot Gris** is popular. **Merlot, Cabernet Franc** and **Pinot Noir** are also used.

Chile
The international varieties, notably **Cabernet Sauvignon, Chardonnay, Sauvignon Blanc** and **Merlot,** dominate plantings in Chile. A notable exception is **Carménère**, which Chile has adopted as its signature red wine variety.

China
Two varieties, **Cabernet Sauvignon** and **Chardonnay**, dominate this emerging giant of the wine world. They comprise well over 80% of plantings.

Croatia
The white wine scene in this country is dominated by Grasevina. Croatia is the point of origin of **Tribidrag**, the variety that Americans call Zinfandel and the

Italians call Primitivo. **Plavic Mali** is a very popular red variety here. It has Tribidrag as one parent. There are many other native varieties reflecting Croatia's long history of viticulture.

France
See separate list below

Georgia
This former Soviet country is not to be confused with the US state. Georgia claims to be the first place where wine was made. It is most famous for being home to the red wine variety **Saperavi**, which is being adopted in may other countries. **Rkatsiteli** dominates the white wine scene, but there are a large numbers of other varieties as befits the country claiming to have the world's oldest wine industry.

Germany
The southern regions are suitable for viticulture, but only for short-growing-season varieties. The characteristic white wines are **Riesling** and **Müller-Thurgau**. **Dornfelder** is the most common red variety; in fact, plantings of this variety are increasing rapidly. Considerable efforts have been made to breed varieties suitable for cooler areas.

Greece
Wine culture is millenniums old in this country. Interestingly, the varietal makeup is still quite idiosyncratic, and growers have largely resisted the trend to plant 'international varieties' seen in many

other old wine-producing areas. Savianto is the most commonly planted white variety. **Xinmavro** and **Agiorgitiko** are the most prominent reds; and there is a variety called Roditis, which comes in red- and grey (pink)-skinned clones.

Hungary
This country is most famous for its Tokaj wines made from the Furmint variety. This variety is also used to make sharpish white wines. Grasevina is a widely grown white wine variety, as is Cserszegi Fuzeres, which also comes in a grey-skinned version. **Blaufränkisch** is the most popular red wine variety.

Italy
See separate list below.

New Zealand
Over the past few decades, New Zealand wine has been dominated by **Sauvignon Blanc**, so that by 2010, that variety made up 50% of the national crop. There are also plantings of **Chardonnay**, and there are increasing amounts of **Pinot Noir** and **Pinot Gris**, but not much else.

Portugal
Many of the varieties which are used to make Port wine are now more commonly used to make dry red wines. The largest plantings of red grapes are of **Tempranillo** (known locally as Tinta Roriz), Touriga Franca, **Touriga Nacionale** and Castelao. Fernao Pires is the most widely planted white wine variety, but the

APPENDIX

more important white wine varieties are **Alvarinho** (Albarino) and Arinto.

Romania
Two native varieties, Feteasca Alba (white) and Fetaesca Regala, dominate the varietal scene in Romania.

South Africa
Chenin Blanc is the long-term favourite white wine variety in South Africa. Its main attraction was its ability to give high yields. Now it is still very popular, but being replaced by **Chardonnay** and **Sauvignon Blanc**. Among the red wines, the most prominent are **Cabernet Sauvignon** and **Merlot**, and there is plenty of the locally bred **Pinotage**.

Spain
The high-yielding white variety Airén long dominated Spanish vineyards. For many years, it was the most planted grape variety in the world based on acreage. It is tough enough to survive the harsh climate of the interior of Spain. The wines are neutral-flavoured at best, and most are distilled for brandy or blended with more desirable varieties. Airén is rapidly being replaced with other varieties. **Verdejo** is a much more highly regarded white variety, and plantings of this are increasing steadily. **Tempranillo** is the ring star, with the area planted of this red variety growing spectacularly. Other common reds are Bobal, **Garnacha** (Grenache) and Monastrell (**Mourvèdre**). **Mencia** has become popular in the UK and elsewhere, but it is still a minor variety in Spain.

United Kingdom
Chardonnay and **Pinot Noir** are popular varieties in the expanding wine industry in the UK. A large proportion of these would be used for sparkling wine. Other varieties commonly used are Bacchus, Seyval Blanc and Reichensteiner.

United States
The white wine scene in the States is dominated by **Chardonnay**. **Sauvignon Blanc** is increasing in area planted. There are many other white varieties, but none represent a significant proportion of the total. Four red wine varieties are prominent: **Cabernet Sauvignon**, **Merlot**, **Tribidrag** (under the name of Zinfandel) and **Pinot Noir**. In the cooler areas, especially in the eastern states, many hybrid varieties are grown, most notably Concord and Norton.

Uruguay
The Uruguayans love to eat beef. That's probably why **Tannat** is so popular. The grape was introduced into Uruguay during the 19th century by a Frenchman from the Basque region. The **Cabernets Sauvignon** and **Franc** and **Merlot** are also prominent among the reds. The Muscat of Hamburg is one of the major whites.

Major Varieties in French wine regions
It is a little meaningless to look at the aggregate varieties for France and Italy because of the huge regional differences.

APPENDIX

Alsace: Gewürztraminer, Pinot Blanc, Pinot Gris, Riesling, Sylvaner, Muscat Blanc (W), Pinot Noir (R).

Bordeaux: Sauvignon Blanc, Semillon, Muscadelle (W), Cabernet Sauvignon, Merlot, Cabernet Franc, Malbec, Petit Verdot (R).

Burgundy: Chardonnay (W), Gamay, Pinot Noir (R).

Champagne: Chardonnay (W), Pinot Noir, Pinot Meunier (R).

Corsica: Vermentino, Chardonnay (W), Sangiovese, Merlot, Cinsaut (R).

Jura: Chardonnay, Savagnin (W), Pinot Noir, Trousseau (R).

Languedoc: Chardonnay, Grenache Blanc, Muscat Blanc (W), Grenache, Syrah, Carignan, Cinsaut, Mourvèdre, Alicante Bouschet (R).

Loire: Muscadet, Chenin Blanc, Sauvignon Blanc (W), Cabernet Franc, Gamay, Grolleau Pinot Noir (R).

Provence: Bourboulenc, Clairette, Grenache Blanc, Marsanne, Viognier (W), **Mourvedre**, Grenache, Cinsaut (R).

Rhone: Marsanne, Roussanne, Viognier, Grenache Blanc (W), Grenache, Syrah, Carignan, Cinsaut, Mourvèdre (R).

Southwest France: Semillon, Sauvignon Blanc, Petit Manseng, Ugni Blanc (W), Tannat, Merlot, Cabernet Franc, Cabernet Sauvignon (R).

WHAT VARIETAL IS THAT?

Major Varieties in Italian wine regions
All of the 21 administrative regions of Italy are also used as the wine regions.

Abbruzzo: Trebbiano (W), Montepulcino (R).

Basilicata: Malvasia, Moscato Bianco (W), Aglianico (R).

Calabria: Greco (W), Gaglioppo (R).

Campania: Coda di Volpe, Falanghina, Fiano, Greco (W), Aglianico, Piedirosso (R).

Emilia-Romagna: Albana, Malvasia, Trebbiano (W), Barbera, Lambrusco.

Friuli-Venezia Giulia: Friulano, Pinot Bianco, Pinot Grigio, Sauvignon Blanc (W), Cabernet Sauvignon, Merlot, Cabernet Franc, Refosco (R).

Lazio: Malvasia, Trebbiano (W), Cesanese, Merlot, Sangiovese (R).

Liguria: Pigato, Vermentino (W), Dolcetto, Rossese (R).

Lombardy: Moscato Bianco, Riesling Italico, Trebbiano (W), Barbera, Bonarda, Nebbiolo, Pinot Noir.

Marche: Trebbiano, Verdiccio (W), Montepulciano, Sangiovese (R).

Molise: Falaghina, Trebbiano (W), Aglianico, Montepulciano (R).

APPENDIX

Piedmont: Arneis, Cortese, Moscato Bianco (W), Barbera, Brachetto, Dolcetto, Nebbiolo.

Puglia: Bianco d'Alessano, Bombino Bianco, Fiano, Trebbiano, Verdeca (W), Nero di Troia (R).

Sardinia: Vermentino (W), Cannonau (Grenache), Carignan, Monica (R).

Sicily: Catarratto Grillo, Inzolia, Malvasia (W), Nero d'Avola, Nerello Mascalese.

Tuscany: Trebbiano, Malvasia, Vernaccia (W), Sangiovese (R).

Trentino-Alto Adige: Gewürztraminer, Müller-Thurgau, Pinot Bianco, Pinot Grigio (W), Lagrein, Marzemino, Pinot Noir, Teroldego.

Umbria: Grecetto, Trebbiano (W), Sagrantino, Sangiovese.

Valle d'Aosta: Blanc de Morgeaux, Petite Arvine, Muscato Bianco (W), Nebbiolo, Furmin.

Veneto: Garganega, Prosecco (W), Corvina, Merlot, Rondinella.

REFERENCES

Anderson, Kym and Nanda R. Ayral. *Which Winegrape Varieties Are Grown Where? A Global Empirical Picture.* University of Adelaide Press, 2013.

Bastianich, Joseph and David Lynch. *Vino Italiano: The Regional Wines of Italy.* New York: Random House, 2005.

Clarke, Oz and Margaret Rand. *Grapes and Wines: A Comprehensive Guide to Varieties and Flavours.* New York: Sterling Epicure, 2015.

d'Agata, Ian. *Native Wine Grapes of Italy.* Berkeley: University of California Press, 2014.

De Long, Deborah and Steve De Long. *De Long's Wine Grape Varietal Table.* London: De Long Company, 2005.

Goldstein, Evan. *Daring Pairings: A Master Sommelier Matches Distinctive Wines with Recipes from His Favorite Chefs.* Berkeley: University of California Press, 2010.

REFERENCES

Robinson, Jancis, Julia Harding and Jose Voulliamoz. *Wine Grapes: A Complete Guide to 1,368 Vine Varieties, Including Their Origin and Flavours.* New York: HarperCollins, 2012.

Further Information

One of the most satisfying thing about wine is that it is always changing. New wine regions, new wineries, new varieties new technologies and new styles are emerging all the time.

A great source of information about the changing Australian wine scene is vinodiversity.com

Specific information and discussion about this book at its Facebook page at www.facebook.com/whatvarietal

About the Author

Darby Higgs is a wine writer based in Melbourne Australia. He is founder of vinodiversity.com the most comprehensive source of information about alternative varietal wines in Australia.

While Darby has no formal wine qualifications he has been exploring the Australian wine industry, especially at the quirky edges for several decades.

Printed in Great Britain
by Amazon